CENTERED

THE SPIRITUALITY
of WORD ON FIRE

ROBERT BARRON

INTRODUCTION *by* JARED ZIMMERER
DIRECTOR *of the* WORD ON FIRE INSTITUTE

Content curated by Bert Ghezzi.

Cover design, typesetting, and interior art direction by Rozann Lee and Cassie Pease.

Unless otherwise noted, Scripture quotations are from the *New Revised Standard Version Bible: Catholic Edition* (copyright © 1989, 1993) National Council of the Churches of Christ in the United States of America. Used by permission. All rights reserved worldwide.

Excerpts from *The Priority of Christ: Toward a Postliberal Catholicism* by Robert Barron (copyright © 2007), *2 Samuel* by Robert Barron (copyright © 2015), *Exploring Catholic Theology: Essays on God, Liturgy, and Evangelization* by Robert Barron (copyright © 2015). All rights reserved. Used with permission of Baker Academic, a division of Baker Publishing Group.

Excerpts from *And Now I See: A Theology of Transformation* by Robert Barron (copyright © 1998), *Thomas Aquinas: Spiritual Master* by Robert Barron (copyright © 2008), *Word on Fire: Proclaiming the Power of Christ* by Robert Barron (copyright © 2008). All rights reserved. Used with permission of The Crossroad Publishing Company, www.crossroadpublishing.com.

Excerpts from *The Strangest Way: Walking the Christian Path* by Robert Barron (copyright © 2002) and *Eucharist* by Robert Barron (copyright © 2008). All rights reserved. Used with permission of Orbis Books.

Excerpts from *Catholicism: A Journey to the Heart of the Faith* by Robert Barron (copyright © 2011), *To Light a Fire on the Earth: Proclaiming the Gospel in a Secular Age* (copyright © 2017). Used by permission of Image Books, an imprint of Random House, a division of Penguin Random House LLC. All rights reserved.

Excerpts from *Seeds of the Word: Finding God in the Culture* by Robert Barron (copyright © 2015), *Vibrant Paradoxes: The Both/And of Catholicism* by Robert Barron (copyright © 2016), *Arguing Religion: A Bishop Speaks at Facebook and Google* by Robert Barron (copyright © 2018). Used with permission of Word on Fire. All rights reserved.

ISBN: 978-1-943243-56-3 (paperback)
ISBN: 978-1-943243-56-3 (eBook)

Library of Congress Control Number: 2020931382
Barron, Robert E., 1959–

Printed in the United States of America

23 22 21 20   1 2 3 4

www.wordonfire.org

CONTENTS

INTRODUCTION

by JARED ZIMMERER

One of the highlights of my life was meeting with the late Cardinal Francis George. Before he passed away, he came to the Word on Fire office in Chicago and met with several people on staff. I was invited by Bishop Barron to join the meeting, even though it was still a few years before I officially joined Word on Fire. I remember Cardinal George asking the very serious question, "Where are the movements in the Church today? Where are the movements that will respond to the spiritual and existential problems of our time?" He was challenging Word on Fire to take its mission to prayer—and through his inspiration, the ministry gave rise to the Word on Fire Institute, a teaching arm designed to form and connect evangelists around the world. It is the beginning of the answer to Cardinal George's call, a response to the most pressing missionary challenge of our time: evangelizing the unaffiliated.

The *Catechism of the Catholic Church* points out that throughout the Church's history, numerous spiritualities have emerged from individual men and women, whose witness to God's love became so compelling that their followers began to share in the same spirit. It continues by stating that a "distinct spirituality can also arise at the point of convergence of liturgical and theological currents, bearing witness to the integration of the faith into a particular human environment and its history." To put this in Balthasarian terms, in the providence of the theo-drama, certain charisms and missions arise to invite people into the divine life. The life and work of Bishop Robert Barron is one such charism, which finds its life in the theological and liturgical current of the Second Vatican Council as properly understood by St. John Paul II, a mission and spirituality that is evangelical to its very core. His spiritual charism is focused on the existential peripheries of our time, combining the best of the theological, philosophical, and mystical traditions of great thinkers and saints.

Centered: The Spirituality of Word on Fire was created as a foundational tool for both the Institute and the broader Word on Fire movement. Its purpose is to help evangelists better understand the spiritual and theological ethos of Word on Fire. You will notice that the contents of this book are aligned with the Eight Principles of Word on Fire. These principles are: unwavering Christocentrism; evangelization of the culture; special commitment to the new media; rooted in the Mystical Body; leading with beauty; affirmative orthodoxy; collaborative apostolate; and grounding in the Eucharist. These pillars are the foundation of every initiative at Word on Fire and will continue shaping its evangelists desiring to better reach the modern world. The beauty of this book is that through the words of our spiritual founder, we can come to contemplate how we can embody these principles ourselves.

The first principle is of significant importance in regard to the spirituality offered by this book. Bishop Barron's first path to holiness is entitled "Finding the Center" in which we revolve the entirety of our being; our relationships, our work, our struggles, our evangelical efforts, around Christ so that we aim each and every aspect to and with the vision of him. The entire mission of the Institute is centered on fulfilling Christ's great call to invite others to participate in the divine life he offers, the life that has changed each of us.

You may also notice that this book is arranged in a blueprint similar to the catechumenate, the process of initiation focused on revelation and the history, beliefs, and practices of the Catholic Church. As the *Catechism* also states, "There is an organic connection between our spiritual life and the dogmas." The catechumenate takes an individual through a journey of discovery, illumination, and ultimately acceptance of the invitation to share in the divine life of Jesus Christ in the sacraments of the Church. In sharing the life of Christ, we must be emboldened to go out; the entire process is teleologically bound to the missionary call of the Gospel. In a way, Bishop Barron is leading his spiritual children through that same process in this book.

Take *Centered* with you to prayer. Reflect on the ways Bishop Barron articulates the truths of Catholicism and allow them to shape your own articulation. Contemplate the ways in which this expression of faith can mold you in the image of

Jesus Christ. Consider it a roadmap by which the ethos and spirituality of Bishop Barron can guide your own daily life of evangelization. Too often we separate our spiritual lives from the life of evangelization. This book will integrate the two.

CHAPTER I

GOD

Precisely because God doesn't need the world,
the very existence of the world is a sign that it
has been loved into being.

Catholicism, 75

BEING ITSELF

Being Itself

The great theologians of the Christian tradition do not typically refer to God as the highest being—which is to say, one being among others, or in David Burrell's phrase, "the biggest thing around." Rather, they tend to use the mysterious and evocative language of "Being itself."

Exploring Catholic Theology, 66

What God Is Like

For the classical theological tradition, God is not a being in the world, one object, however supreme, among many. The maker of the entire universe cannot be, himself, an item within the universe, and the one who is responsible for the nexus of causal relations in its entirety could never be a missing link in an ordinary scientific schema. Thomas Aquinas makes the decisive point when he says that God is not *ens summum* (highest being) but rather *ipsum esse* (the sheer act of Being itself). God is neither a thing in the world, nor the sum total of existing things; he is instead the unconditioned cause of the conditioned universe, the reason why there is something rather than nothing. Accordingly, God is not some good thing, but Goodness itself;

3

not some true object, but Truth itself; not some beautiful reality, but Beauty itself.

Seeds of the Word, 233–234

Beyond the Genus of Being

Aquinas goes so far as to say that God cannot be defined or situated within any genus, even the genus of "being." This means that it is wrong to say that trees, planets, automobiles, computers, and God—despite the obvious differences among them—have at least in common their status as beings.

Catholicism, 63

The Serenity of God

In his *Dogmatik* of 1925, Paul Tillich speaks of the *Klarheit* (clarity) possessed by God, and in his *Summa theologiae*, Thomas Aquinas speaks of God's characteristic attribute of simplicity, and in his *Church Dogmatics*, Karl Barth insists upon the *Gottheit Gottes* (the Godliness of God). All three theologians are describing what I have chosen to call the serenity of the divine reality. In one sense, God is like the clear unbroken surface of an unroiled sea, or like a single Doric column rising into a cloudless sky, or like a pure solo soprano voice singing the simplest of melodies. There is a peaceful untrammeled serenity to the divine being, since God is the sheer act of existence. As the sacred name "I am who I am" (Exod. 3:14) suggests, God is not this or that kind of being, not this or that particular deity, but rather the act of Being itself. There is therefore something clean, pure, untroubled, and uncomplicated about the divine reality.

And Now I See, 133–134

Continuously Creating

Creation is not a once-and-for-all act of the essentially transcendent God, but rather the ever-present and ever-new gift of being poured out from the divine source. Thomas Aquinas describes creation in an unusually poetic way as *quaedam relatio ad Creatorem cum novitate essendi* (a kind of relationship to the Creator with freshness of being). What he implies is that the creature *is a relationship* to the energy of God, which is continually drawing it from nonbeing to being, making it new. When Jesus speaks to the Samaritan woman at the well and promises her "water gushing up to eternal life" (John 4:14), he evokes what Aquinas means by creation: the presence of God always at work at the very roots of our being.

And Now I See, 141

The Best Argument for God's Existence

You and I are contingent (dependent) in our being in the measure that we eat and drink, breathe, and had parents; a tree is contingent inasmuch as its being is derived from seed, sun, soil, water, etc.; the solar system is contingent because it depends upon gravity and events in the wider galaxy. To account for a contingent reality, by definition we have to appeal to an extrinsic cause. But if that cause is itself contingent, we have to proceed further. This process of appealing to contingent causes in order to explain a contingent effect cannot go on indefinitely, for then the effect is never adequately explained. Hence, we must finally come to some reality that is not contingent on anything else, some ground of being whose very nature is to-be. This is precisely what Catholic theology means by "God."

To Light a Fire on the Earth, 195–196

Our Transcendent and Immanent God

The Gothic cathedrals of the Middle Ages expressed in stone and glass an eloquent ambiguity in the assigning of names to God. I would draw your attention—to give just one example— to the mountainous cathedral that looms over the Rhine River in Cologne, Germany and dominates, even today, the skyline of the city. Every line on the exterior of the building points dramatically upward; the logic of the structure compels the viewer's gaze skyward; the sheer immensity of it makes it hard to take in. I can personally witness to the fact that vertigo sets in as one tries to comprehend its dimensions. All of this speaks of the transcendence, strangeness, and radical otherness of God. The building is telling us that whatever idea we have of God has to be abandoned as inadequate; it is summoning us always to look higher. But the same Cologne Cathedral, which speaks so compellingly of the divine transcendence, preaches just as convincingly the immanence of God. All over the surface of the structure—but especially around the portals—one spies plants, animals, trees, planets, the sun and moon, angels, devils, and saints—the whole panoply of creation, both natural and supernatural, vividly portrayed. All of these creatures have to do with God, and God has to do with all of them.

Catholicism, 73–74

NOT *a* COMPETITOR

Union with God

The proximity of God is not a threat to a creature but, on the contrary, that which allows the creature to be most fully itself. If a fellow creature were to enter into the very constitution of my being, I would be the victim of an aggression, and my freedom and integrity would be undermined. But the true God can enter into the most intimate ontological unity with a creature, and the result is not diminution but enhancement of creaturely being. God and the worldly are therefore capable of an ontological coinherence, a being-in-the-other, so that each can let the other be even as they enter into the closest contact.

The Priority of Christ, 56

Not a Competitor

The Incarnation tells central truths concerning both God and us. If God became human without ceasing to be God and without compromising the integrity of the creature that he became, God must not be a competitor with his creation. In many of the ancient myths and legends, divine figures such as Zeus or Dionysus enter into human affairs only through aggression, destroying or wounding that which they invade.

Catholicism, 1–2

7

The Divine Difference

If in Jesus a divine and human nature come together non-competitively in ontological unity, there must be something altogether different about the divine nature. The divine way of being must not be a worldly nature, one type of creaturely being among many; rather, it must be *somehow else*. The difference between divinity and creatureliness must be a noncontrastive difference, unlike that which obtains between finite things. God is indeed other than any worldly nature, but he is, if I can put it this way, *otherly other*. Nicholas of Cusa expressed this paradox neatly when he said that God is both *totaliter aliter* (totally other) and the *Non-Aliud* (the non-other).

The Priority of Christ, 55

On Fire But Not Burned Up

Stealing the fire, which was the unique preserve of the gods, Prometheus aroused the wrath of Zeus and suffered the grim fate of having his liver chewed out and eaten daily by an eagle. In the desperate zero-sum game of classical mythology, human flourishing is an affront to the gods and must be punished. And then there is the Bible. When the true God—the God Who Is, the God whose essence is identical to his existence—comes close to creatures, they are not consumed; rather, they become more beautifully and radiantly themselves, on fire but not burned up. This theme runs through the whole Bible and was given splendid expression by St. Paul who said, in an ecstatic exclamation, "It is no longer I who live, but it is Christ who lives in me" (Gal. 2:20). Though his entire existence was taken over by Jesus Christ, Paul is not less himself; he is, instead, the richest version of himself.

Arguing Religion, 105–106

DIVINE LOVE

Why God *Is* Love

There must be within the structure of the divine to-be a play of giver, gift, and giving. Prior to the event of Jesus Christ, it might have been possible to see that God, due to the simplicity of his existence, could give with unalloyed generosity to creatures, but it was not possible to see that the divine being is itself a play of generosity. That God loves can follow from the simplicity of his being and the fact of creation, but that he *is* love appears to us only through the icon of the Incarnation and its display of a manifold within the divine reality. Now we begin to see more clearly: what the simple God gives with utter generosity is the giving that he is. The to-be of God is to-give, is to-be-for-the-other.

The Priority of Christ, 238

Seeds of the Trinitarian Doctrine

Though a fully developed doctrine of the Trinity is not explicitly presented in Scripture, the New Testament is filled with the seeds from which that doctrine would eventually grow. At the end of Matthew's Gospel, the risen Jesus commands his disciples to spread the Good News to all nations and to baptize people in the name of the Father, the Son, and the Holy Spirit. Sprinkled throughout the Pauline literature are references to the triunity of God: in the letter to the Romans, Paul reminds us that the Father has sent his Son in the fullness of time in order that we might all become his sons and daughters, and he specifies that it is only in the Spirit that we can call God "Abba" or Father. All of this New Testament witness to the triune nature of God is summed up in the implicitly trinitarian formula in 1 John 4:16: "God is love." If love is not simply an activity in which the one God engages but rather what God essentially is, then God must be in his nature a play of lover, beloved, and active love.

The Priority of Christ, 240

A Family of Persons

There is in God a play of lover and beloved; but the lover and beloved are connected by the love they have in common. Therefore, the God disclosed in Jesus is a family or community of persons: Father, Son, and Spirit. The ground of being is not a thing or a monolith or an absolute; rather, it is a *communio* of being and letting be. From all eternity, the Father forgets about himself in love and generates the Son, and from all eternity, the Son forgets about himself and looks to the Father, and the mutual love of Father and Son is the Holy Spirit. Active generation, passive generation; active spiration, passive spiration. Breathing in and breathing out; being and letting-be. God is like a set of lungs, or like a heart—taking in and letting out, a rhythm, a cadence, a back-and-forth of love.

"Moving Beyond a Beige Catholicism," Talk

To Make Love Real

The one God of Israel, "I am who I am" (Exod. 3:14), is a play of subsistent relations—"God is love" (1 John 4:16)—and thus we learn the deepest meaning of the verb to be is "to love." It was the Son, the Father's beloved, who became incarnate in Jesus, and it was the Holy Spirit, the love breathed back and forth between the Father and the Son, that came to dwell in the Church. And the Church's mission, therefore, is to make real in the world precisely this love that God is.

Catholicism, 87

God's Unselfish Love

God cannot be caught in an economic exchange because he can in no ontologically real way benefit from either our gifts or our gratitude; nor can he be hurt by the lack thereof. Because he is not, as Thomas Aquinas put it, really related to the world, God can—indeed must—give in a totally non-self-interested manner, and if love means willing the good of the other as other, then God's acts of self-offering on behalf of the world are loving in the fullest possible sense. Further, whatever gift is given back to God by a creature must necessarily redound to the benefit of the creature, since it cannot add to the divine being. The gifts of God, therefore, even as they awaken gratitude in those who receive them, involve neither party in the vicious cycle of a mutually obliging economic exchange; rather, they ground a loop or cycle of grace between the divine and the nondivine.

Bridging the Great Divide, 47

Loved into Being

Precisely because God doesn't need the world, the very existence of the world is a sign that it has been loved into being.

Catholicism, 75

Out of Nothing, Out of Love

In all of the philosophies and mythologies of the ancient world, creation takes place through some act of violence or domination—the chaos, matter, other gods, or principles are subdued through a greater act of violence on the part of the most powerful god. There is none of this in Christianity. The true God creates *ex nihilo*, literally from nothing, implying that there is nothing standing outside of God, nothing that needs to be mastered, overcome, manipulated, or dominated. Rather, in a sheer, unimaginably generous act, God makes the world out of nothing and out of love.

"Moving Beyond a Beige Catholicism," Talk

A Nonviolent, Relational God

The crucified Jesus returned alive to those who had abused, abandoned, denied, and fled from him, but he confronted them not with threats and vengeance but with the nonviolence of compassion and forgiveness. The moral disorder produced by the Crucifixion of the Son of God was restored not through a violent imposition of divine retributive justice but through restorative divine forgiveness, not through a suppression of will by Will but by an insinuating invitation to love. On the basis of this luminous revelation, Christians concluded the nonviolent and relational character of God's own being. God is not so much a monolith of power and ontological perfection as a play of love and relationality. The author of the first letter of John stated this revolutionary insight with admirable laconicism: "God is love" (1 John 4:16).

The Priority of Christ, 17–18

CHAPTER II

JESUS CHRIST

Christianity asserts that the infinite and the finite
met, that the eternal and the temporal embraced, that
the fashioner of the galaxies and planets became a
baby too weak even to raise his head.

Catholicism, 9

UNWAVERING CHRISTOCENTRISM

The Someone at the Center

One of the most important things to understand about Christianity is that it is not primarily a philosophy or a system of ethics or a religious ideology. It is a relationship to the unsettling person of Jesus Christ, to the God-man. Some*one* stands at the center of Christian concern. Though Christian thinkers have used philosophical ideas and cultural constructs to articulate the meaning of the faith—sometimes in marvelously elaborate ways—they never, at their best, wander far from the very particular and unnerving first-century rabbi from Nazareth.

Catholicism, 10

The Lord of All

To be sure, Christians should never enter the public arena violently, aggressively, or in meanness of spirit, for such a move would undermine the very principles we are endeavoring to propagate. But we should do so boldly and confidently, for we are not announcing a private or personal spirituality, but rather declaring a new King under whose lordship *everything* must fall. If Jesus is truly Lord, then government, business, family life, the arts, sexuality, and entertainment all come properly under his headship.

"Imago Dei as Privilege and Mission," Talk

The Power Source

Christianity is, first and foremost, a religion of the concrete and not the abstract. It takes its power not from a general religious consciousness, not from an ethical conviction, not from a comfortable abstraction, but from the person Jesus Christ. It is Christ—in his uncompromising call to repentance, his unforgettable gestures of healing, his unique and disturbing praxis of forgiveness, his provocative nonviolence and especially his movement from godforsakenness and death to shalom-radiating Resurrection—that moves the believer to change of life and gift of self.

Bridging the Great Divide, 19–20

THE INCARNATION

The Catholic Thing

What is the Catholic thing? What makes Catholicism, among all of the competing philosophies, ideologies, and religions of the world, distinctive? I stand with John Henry Newman who said that *the* great principle of Catholicism is the Incarnation, the enfleshment of God. What do I mean by this? I mean, *the Word of God*—the mind by which the whole universe came to be— did not remain sequestered in heaven but rather entered into this ordinary world of bodies, this grubby arena of history, this compromised and tear-stained human condition of ours. "The Word became flesh and lived among us" (John 1:14): that is the Catholic thing.

Catholicism, 1

God Became a Baby

The central claim of Christianity—still startling after two thousand years—is that God *became* human. The Creator of the cosmos, who transcends any definition or concept, took to himself a nature like ours, *becoming* one of us. Christianity asserts that the infinite and the finite met, that the eternal and the temporal embraced, that the fashioner of the galaxies and planets became a baby too weak even to raise his head.

Catholicism, 9

The Great Exchange

The Logos became flesh, our flesh, so that we might allow the divine energy to come to birth in us. Much of this is summed up in the oft-repeated patristic adage that God became human that humans might become God.

Bridging the Great Divide, 238

Reflecting Christ's Light

The declaration of Mary as Mother of God is an instance of the general principle that whatever is said about Mary is meant not so much to draw attention to her as to throw light on Christ. To say that Mary is the Mother of God is to insist on the density of the claim that God truly became human, one of us, bone of our bone and flesh of our flesh. As Fulton J. Sheen commented, Mary is like the moon, for her light is always the reflection of a higher light.

Catholicism, 97–98

Food for a Hungry World

The account of Jesus' birth in the Gospel of Luke is not, as Raymond E. Brown reminded us, an innocent tale that we tell to children. Instead, we are meant to notice a contrast between the figure mentioned at the outset of the narrative—Caesar Augustus—and the character who is at the center of the story. Caesar would have been the best-fed person in the ancient world. But the true king, the true emperor of the world, is born in a cave outside of a forgotten town on the verge of Caesar's domain. Too weak even to raise his head, he is wrapped in swaddling clothes and then laid "in a manger" (Luke 2:7), the place where the animals eat. What Luke is signaling here is that Jesus had come to be food for a hungry world. Whereas Caesar—in the manner of Eve and Adam—existed to be fed, Jesus existed to be fed upon. He was destined to be not only the host at the sacred banquet but the meal itself.

Eucharist, 39

A Balance of Extremes

Chesterton commented that a mark of the Catholic Church is a holding together of opposing elements in creative tension: asceticism and sensuality, divine immanence and divine transcendence, procreation and celibacy, etc. This characteristic style is grounded in the great paradox of the Incarnation, which is a coming together of divinity and humanity without mixing, mingling, or confusion. The Church likes, Chesterton concluded, red and white, though "it has always had a healthy hatred of pink." So it presents an extreme, even exaggerated, moral demand *and* an extreme, even exaggerated, mercy.

"*Imago Dei* as Privilege and Mission," Talk

The Coinherence between Divinity and Humanity

If the Incarnation is an accomplished fact, then the presence of the true God is not invasive or interruptive but rather noncompetitive. In light of this coming together, we must say that there is a rapport of coinherence between divinity and humanity, each abiding in the other in such a way that humanity is elevated by the proximity of the divine. St. Irenaeus summed up this radical idea in the pithy formula *Gloria Dei homo vivens* (the glory of God is a human being fully alive).

The Priority of Christ, 17

Touched by Divine Power

The Incarnation means that nothing of our humanity is alien to God or untouched by divine power: birth, coming of age, rejection, triumph, friendship, betrayal, anxiety, bliss, the frightful darkness of death—all of it becomes, in principle, a route of access to the transcendent reality. Because of the coming together of the divine and human in Jesus, we have the courage to explore a new and deeper identity, one rooted not in the petty desires and fears of the ego, but in the eternal power and existence of God.

Bridging the Great Divide, 238

Participating in the Incarnation

I echo the great medieval mystic Meister Eckhart in saying that if the Word does not come to birth in us today, it is no use reading about the Incarnation of that Word in a person long ago. If, in short, we ourselves do not *participate* in who Jesus was, we miss the spiritual power that he meant to unleash. If John's Gospel is any indication, Jesus does not want worshipers but followers, or better, *participants*: "I am the vine, you are the branches" (John 15:5); "Those who eat my flesh and drink my blood abide in me, and I in them" (John 6:56). The beautifully organic images that John presents are meant, it seems to me, to communicate the life-changing power of the Incarnation.

Bridging the Great Divide, 238

The Energy of the Incarnation

To live in the energy of the Incarnation is to know that real union with God, in the depth of our humanity, is not simply a hope or a wild dream but a concrete possibility. Jesus Christ, the incarnate Word, shows to the world that the human being is made for God and finds rest only in God. More to the point, Jesus reveals that God wants nothing more than to come to life in us, to become incarnate in our words and actions, in our thoughts, fears, and insecurities.

Bridging the Great Divide, 238

DEATH *and* RESURRECTION

Why the Crucifixion Was Necessary

The scriptural authors understand sin not so much as a series of acts but as a condition in which we are stuck, something akin to an addiction or a contagious disease. No amount of merely human effort could possibly solve the problem. Rather, some power has to come from outside of us in order to clean up the mess; something awful has to be done on our behalf in order to offset the awfulness of sin. With this biblical realism in mind, we can begin to comprehend why the Crucifixion of the Son of God was necessary.

"How Strange Is the Cross of Christ," Article

The Unsurpassable Punishment

We are the inheritors of centuries of artwork and piety that present the cross as a moving, or even saccharine, religious symbol. But for the men and women of Jesus' time, death by crucifixion was not only painful; it was brutally dehumanizing, humiliating, and shaming. A person condemned to this manner of execution would be stripped naked, nailed or tied to a cross-bar fitted into a stake, and then left for hours—or in many cases, days—to suffer the excruciating (*ex cruce*, literally "from the cross") pain of very slowly asphyxiating while rocking up and down on wounded hands and feet in order to respirate. The mocking of the crucified, which is frankly described in the Gospels, was part and parcel of the execution. When at long last the tortured criminal died, his body was allowed to remain on the cross for days, permitting animals to pick over his remains. Jesus' rapid burial was exceptional, a favor specially offered to Joseph of Arimathea, a high-ranking Jewish official. We can clearly see why Cicero referred to crucifixion, with admirable laconicism, as the *summum suplicium* (the unsurpassable punishment).

"How Strange Is the Cross of Christ," Article

A Prophetic Sign

Over his cross, Pontius Pilate had placed a sign announcing in Hebrew, Latin, and Greek that Jesus was the king of the Jews. Though Pilate meant it as mockery, it was in fact the fulfillment of a prophecy. An essential aspect of the hope of Israel was that one day a king in the tradition of David and Solomon would rise up, take his place in Jerusalem, and deal definitively with the enemies of the nation. This is precisely who Jesus was and precisely what Jesus did.

Eucharist, 84

Shielded by Christ

In the Gospel of Luke, Jesus compared himself to a mother hen who longed to gather her chicks under her wing. As N.T.

Wright points out, this is much more than a sentimental image. It refers to the gesture of a hen when fire is sweeping through the barn. In order to protect her chicks, she will sacrifice herself, gathering them under her wing and using her own body as a shield. On the cross, Jesus used, as it were, his own sacrificed body as a shield, taking the full force of the world's hatred and violence. He entered into close quarters with sin (because that's where we sinners are found) and allowed the heat and fury of sin to destroy him, even as he protected us.

Eucharist, 84

The Easter Revolution

The Easter declaration, properly understood, has always been and still is an explosion, an earthquake, a revolution. For the Easter faith—on clear display from the earliest days of the Christian movement—is that Jesus of Nazareth, a first-century Jew from the northern reaches of the Promised Land, who had been brutally put to death by the Roman authorities, is alive again through the power of the Holy Spirit. And not alive, I hasten to add, in some vague or metaphorical sense. That the Resurrection is a literary device or a symbol that Jesus' cause goes on is a fantasy born in the faculty lounges of Western universities over the past couple of centuries. The still startling claim of the first witnesses is that Jesus rose bodily from death, presenting himself to his disciples to be seen, even handled.

"The Startlingly Good News of the Resurrection," Article

Judgment on Jesus' Opponents

Once we've come to some clarity about the Resurrection claim itself, we can begin to see why it still matters so massively. Let us look at the kerygmatic sermon that St. Peter preached in the Jerusalem temple in the days immediately following Pentecost. "The God of Abraham, the God of Isaac, and the God of Jacob . . . has glorified his servant Jesus, whom you handed over and rejected in the presence of Pilate . . . You killed the author of life" (Acts 3:13, 15). The Resurrection is being presented here as an affirmation of Jesus to be sure, but also as a judgment on those who stood opposed to Jesus. St. Peter holds it up as the surest sign possible that God stands athwart the injustice, stupidity, and cruelty of the world and its leaders.

"The Startlingly Good News of the Resurrection," Article

The Marriage of Heaven and Earth

A great implication of the Resurrection is that heaven and earth are coming together. Many Christians today remain haunted by the Platonic view that matter and spirit are opponents and that the purpose of life is finally to affect a prison-break, releasing the soul from the body. This might have been Plato's philosophy, but it has precious little to do with the Bible. The hope of ancient Israel was not a jail-break, not an escape from this world, but precisely the unification of heaven and earth in a great marriage. Recall a central line from the prayer that Jesus bequeathed to his Church: "Thy kingdom come, thy will be done, *on earth as it is in heaven*." The bodily Resurrection of Jesus—the "first fruits of those who have died" (1 Cor. 15:20)—is the powerful sign that the two orders are in fact coming together.

"The Startlingly Good News of the Resurrection," Article

CHAPTER III

LIFE *in* CHRIST

Happiness is never a function of filling oneself up;
it is a function of giving oneself away.
Arguing Religion, 98

THE PRIORITY
of GRACE

God Is After Us

Biblical religion is not primarily about our quest for God; it is about God's quest for us. For the authors of the Bible, the interesting thing is not that we seek joy and spiritual fulfillment. The interesting thing is that God seeks us with a reckless abandon.

"The Pursuing God," Homily

Divine Life on the Fly

When the divine grace enters one's life (and everything we have is the result of divine grace), the task is to contrive a way to make it a gift. In a sense, the divine life—which exists only in gift form—can be "had" only on the fly. When we try to make it our own possession, it necessarily evanesces, for it can't exist in that manner.

Arguing Religion, 99

Conformed to the Way of Love

In imitation of our first parents, we have tried to fill up the emptiness with wealth, pleasure, power, honor, the sheer love of domination—but none of it works, precisely because we have all been wired for God and God *is* nothing but love. It is only when we conform ourselves to the way of love, only when, in a high paradox, we contrive to empty out the ego, that we are filled.

Eucharist, 43

What Makes Real Love Possible

Love is described in the Christian tradition as a theological virtue—which is to say, a habit or capacity that comes not from the cultivation of natural potentialities but as a gift from God. This is true because love is a participation in the divine life. The simple Creator God is uniquely capable of love in the complete sense, since he alone can fully will the good of the other as other. The real giving of gifts is practically impossible among us creatures, compromised as we are by ontological neediness, self-interest, and violence. What makes real love possible among humans is only a sharing in the love with which God loves, some participation in the divine to-be. When we root ourselves in the God who has no need, who exists in radical self-sufficiency, we can begin to love the other as he does, for our needy, grasping ego has been transfigured by proximity to the divine way of life.

The Priority of Christ, 234

The Conduit to Grace

God's grace and loving kindness are neither manipulative nor domineering; instead, they require, by God's design, the conduit of a receptive freedom in order to be realized into our lives. It is a commonplace of Catholic theology that God is always pleased to work in cooperation with our powers of will and mind. Faith, therefore, is this conduit, this open door; it is a signal, coming from the depths of our existence, that we want to cooperate with grace.

Word on Fire, 164

The Loop of Grace

God's love can truly dwell in us and become our "possession" only in the measure that we give it away. If we resist it or try to cling to it, it will never work its way into our own hearts, bodies, and minds. But if we give it away as an act of love, then we get more of it, entering into a delightful stream of grace. If you give away the divine love, then you keep it. Then it "remains" in you.

"Love Both Conditional and Unconditional," Homily

Happiness Is Giving Oneself Away

The most important, though highly paradoxical, principle of spiritual physics holds that the infinite God alone can satisfy the infinite hunger of the heart, and therefore, only when the soul is filled by God will it find beatitude. But who is God? According to the teaching at the very heart of Christianity, God is love. God is self-diffusive gift. Therefore, to be filled with God is to be filled with love—which is to say, the willingness to empty oneself for the sake of the other. And so the paradox: happiness is never a function of filling oneself up; it is a function of giving oneself away.

Arguing Religion, 98–99

PRAYER

Being with God

Prayer is being with God, becoming attuned to God, thinking his thoughts and feeling his feelings.

Catholicism, 225

Prayer Expands Our Hearts

According to St. Augustine, God wants us to ask, seek, and petition persistently, not in order that he might be changed but that we might be changed. Through the initial refusal to give us what we want, God compels our hearts to expand in order to receive adequately what he wants to give. In the very process of hungering and thirsting for certain goods, we make ourselves worthy vessels. It is not as though in petitioning God we are approaching a stubborn pasha or big city boss who we hope might be persuaded by our persistence. Rather, it is God who works a sort of spiritual alchemy in us by forcing us to wait.

Catholicism, 245

God Delights in Our Requests

If God cannot change, what is the point of asking him for anything? And if God is omniscient, what is the point of telling him what you need? Keep in mind that the same Jesus who told us to ask and ask again also informed us that God "knows what you need before you ask him" (Matt. 6:8). One way to shed light on this problem is to refer to the biblical master metaphor for God—namely, the parent. Parents hear petitions from their children constantly, persistent requests for things, some good and some quite bad—and decent parents know what their child needs long before she asks for it. But none of this conduces a parent toward stifling those requests or pronouncing them useless—even if he is obliged frequently to respond negatively. God indeed knows everything about everything, so he is aware of what we need before we ask; yet still, like a good parent, he delights in hearing our requests—and like a good parent, does not always respond the way we would like him to.

Catholicism, 244–245

The Family, a School of Prayer

St. Pope John Paul II urged us to see the family as an *ecclesiola* (a little church)—which is to say, a place where people learn to pray and to make God the absolute center of their lives. The rosary, morning and evening prayers, blessings of children as they go off to bed, regular attendance at Mass and participation in the other sacraments—through all these practices, families develop as schools of prayer. One cannot help but think in this context of the manner in which Karol Wojtyla's father, by his quiet but consistent piety, shaped his son to be saint who would, in time, transform the face of the earth.

"*Imago Dei* as Privilege and Mission," Talk

The Coming Together of Two Longings

St. John of Damascus, a monk and theologian from the eighth century, said, "Prayer is the raising of one's mind and heart to God," and St. Thérèse of Lisieux said that "prayer is a surge of the heart; it is a simple look turned toward heaven, it is a cry of recognition and of love." Prayer is born of that awareness, felt more than thought, that the transcendent realm impinges on our lowly world and hence can be contacted. A basic Christian conviction is that this reaching for God meets an even more passionate divine reaching for us. Perhaps we would put it best by saying that the mystical coming together of these two longings—our longing for God and God's longing for us—is prayer.

Catholicism, 224–225

A NEW WAY
of LIVING

Seeing Things Differently

Christianity is, above all, a way of *seeing*. Everything else in Christian life flows from and circles around the transformation of vision. Christians *see* differently, and that is why their prayer, their worship, their action, their whole way of being in the world have a distinctive accent and flavor. What unites figures as diverse as James Joyce, Caravaggio, John Milton, Thomas Aquinas, the architect of Chartres, Dorothy Day, Dietrich Bonhoeffer, and the later Bob Dylan is a peculiar and distinctive *take* on things, a style, a way, which flow finally from Jesus of Nazareth.

And Now I See, 1

Living the Supernatural Life

In John 15, Jesus declares that he is the vine and we are the branches. He is the power and energy source in which we live. This image is closely related to Paul's metaphor of the Body of Christ. The point is that we live in him and he in us. Jesus is the source of supernatural life in us, and without him, we would have none of it. If, therefore, you are separated from the vine, you will die spiritually; you will stop living a supernatural life. What does this look like concretely, to be attached to the vine? It means a steady immersion in the prayer of the Church. It means steady communion with God, speaking to him on a regular basis. It means an immersion in the Scriptures, soaking in the truth of the Bible. It means engaging in the corporal and spiritual works of mercy. And, of course, it means you must participate in the sacraments—especially Confession and the Eucharist. By the sacraments, we stay close to the Christ who forgives our sins and who enlivens our spirits.

"The Vine and the Branches," Homily

The Grace of Love

Love is not primarily a feeling or an instinct; rather, it is the act of willing the good of the other as other. It is radical self-gift, living for the sake of the other. To be kind to someone else so that he might be kind to you, or to treat a fellow human being justly so that he, in turn, might treat you with justice, is not to love, for such moves are tantamount to indirect self-interest. Truly to love is to move outside of the black hole of one's egotism, to resist the centripetal force that compels one to assume the attitude of self-protection. But this means that love is rightly described as a "theological virtue," for it represents a participation in the love that God is. Since God has no needs, only God can utterly exist for the sake of the other. All of the great masters of the Christian spiritual tradition saw that we are able to love only inasmuch as we have received, as a grace, a share in the very life, energy, and nature of God.

Seeds of the Word, 230–231

The Truth About Enemies

Enemies are also our brothers and our sisters. Notice please that I am not denying that we have enemies, real enemies, who are wicked, twisted, violent, and dangerous. But it is a Christian conviction that all of that evil is not telling the deepest truth about the enemy. The deepest truth is that he or she is a child of God, and thus worthy of our love.

Seeds of the Word, 221

"Forgive" Is an Active Verb

For Christians, forgiveness is not simply an attitude or an inner state or a decision; it is an action. To forgive is actively to reconcile, to repair a ruptured relationship, bearing the burden of another. It is, by definition, to go beyond justice.

"Moving Beyond a Beige Catholicism," Talk

Turn the Other Cheek

In both the animal kingdom and among human beings, two standard responses to violence can be discerned: fight or flight. In the Sermon on the Mount, Jesus indicates a third way beyond fighting or fleeing, a way of engaging the wicked so as to move them to conversion. To turn the other cheek, accordingly, is not acquiescence or surrender; rather, it is a mirroring technique, which compels the aggressor to see his aggression. In the martial art form called aikido, the warrior does not aggress his opponent, but rather uses his opponent's weight and momentum against him. As one proponent of this method explained once to me, the purpose of the aikido warrior is not to injure or kill his counterpart, but instead to leave him laughing on the floor. I would suggest that what Jesus proposes in the Sermon on the Mount is a kind of spiritual and moral aikido, a creative and nonviolent way to engage the violence of the world.

"Imago Dei as Privilege and Mission," Talk

The Mercy Connection

The corporal works of mercy signal the fact that we are connected to each other in God whether we like it or not, and they act out that fact.

"Moving Beyond a Beige Catholicism," Talk

DISCIPLESHIP

Staying with Jesus

When, at the beginning of John's Gospel, two of John the Baptist's disciples approach Jesus, the Lord turns round on them and asks, "What are you looking for?" They do not respond as we might expect, requesting wisdom or direction or insight. Instead, they answer the question with another question: "Where are you staying?" (John 1:38). The term "stay" (*menein*) is replete with spiritual overtones in the fourth Gospel. It indicates where someone roots himself, where he derives his spiritual power. Hence, "My Father will love them, and we will come to them and make our home with them" (John 14:23) and "I am in the Father and the Father is in me" (John 14:11). So the disciples, in inquiring where he stays, are asking Jesus *about himself*, to show them the source of his life. Obviously pleased with their question, Jesus says, "Come and see" (John 1:39). They will find what they seek—not simply by listening to his speech but by watching him at close quarters, moving in with him, participating in his world. So the one who today seeks to understand Jesus cannot be content with either religious abstraction or historical archaeology; rather, she must stay with him. She must enter into his distinctive way of being, as this has been made available through the dense tangle of the biblical narratives.

The Priority of Christ, 50

The Conditions of Discipleship

For all of us sinners, to varying degrees, our own lives have become god. That is to say, we see the universe turning around our ego, our needs, our projects, our plans, and our likes and dislikes. True conversion—the *metanoia* that Jesus talks about—is so much more than moral reform, though it includes that. It has to do with a complete shift in consciousness, a whole new way of looking at one's life. Jesus offered a teaching that must have been gut-wrenching to his first-century audience: "If any want to become my followers, let them deny themselves and take up their cross daily and follow me" (Luke 9:23). His listeners knew what the cross meant: a death in utter agony, nakedness, and humiliation. They didn't think of the cross automatically in religious terms, as we do. They knew it in all of its awful power. Unless you crucify your ego, you cannot be my follower, Jesus says. This move—this terrible move—has to be the foundation of the spiritual life.

"The Awful Gospel of the Cross," Homily

Apprenticeship Needed

Christianity, the way of Jesus Christ, *is* a culture, a style of life supported by a unique set of convictions, assumptions, hopes, and practices. It is like a game with a unique texture, feel, and set of rules. As such, it is a milieu into which one must be introduced through a process of practice and *apprenticeship.*

Bridging the Great Divide, 22

A Disciple's Practical Service

When idealistic young people came to the Catholic Worker House in New York, full of romantic fantasies about being with the poor, Dorothy Day always told them, "There are two things you should know about the poor: they tend to smell and they are ungrateful." What she was communicating to them was the hard truth that the corporal and spiritual works of mercy cost—and that they will mark the body and soul. These exercises, these practices, are, I think, ways of apprenticing to the Master, means of access to the culture of Christianity.

Bridging the Great Divide, 29

The True Identity of a Disciple

Before he calls Matthew to do anything, before he sends him on mission, Jesus invites Matthew to recline in easy fellowship around a festive table. Erasmo Leiva-Merikakis comments, "The deepest meaning of Christian discipleship is not to work for Jesus but to be with Jesus." The former tax-collector listens to the Word, laughs with him, breaks bread with him, and in this finds his true identity. Adam was the friend of Yahweh before becoming, through his own fear and pride, Yahweh's enemy. Now Jesus, Yahweh made flesh, seeks to reestablish this lost friendship with Adam's descendants.

Eucharist, 40–41

Following Jesus to Calvary

Dietrich Bonhoeffer commented that when the Lord summons a person to discipleship he calls to him to come and die. When

43

the blind Bartimaeus received his sight, at the midpoint of the Gospel of Mark, he followed Jesus up the road that would lead to Calvary. The way which is the Christian life begins and ends with the man who is God dying on a cross.

The Strangest Way, 166–167

CHAPTER IV

REVELATION

In the fullness of time, God spoke, as the author
of the letter to the Hebrews has it, "by a Son" (Heb. 1:2).
Arguing Religion, 12

SCRIPTURE

Approaching God's Library

People often think that the Bible's a book. I always say, begin with the etymology of the word *Bible*—it's *Ta Biblia*, "the books." It's not a book; it's a library. Then my next move is typically to ask, "Do you take the whole library literally?" Well, it depends on what section you're in. You're wandering around the library, and some of the books are relatively straightforward. Then you wander into the poetry section, the mythology section, the fiction section, and things are different. We're dealing with books here with widely different authors, genres, audiences, purposes, and so on. To make sense of it all, you have to read it within an interpretive tradition. You don't just pick it up and start reading it. It's like saying, "Here's *Hamlet*, knock yourself out." No, you'd say, "Read *Hamlet* within this long tradition of interpretation, and then you begin to understand it." In the same way, with the books of the Bible you need so much contextualization.

To Light a Fire on the Earth, 170

The Bible Read from God's Perspective

Since the Bible is the story of God's dealings with creation, the Scriptures themselves participate in the divine Logos, and particular parts of Scripture participate in one another, contributing to the whole of divine revelation. The Bible, consequently, ought never to be read simply as a congeries of unrelated tales, prophecies, histories, and words of wisdom, drawn from a variety of sources and in response to differing historical situations. Though it might seem that way "from the ground," it takes on coherence and consistency when read from the standpoint of the divine author. Thus, the Bible is a *symphonos*, a sounding together of tones and melodies, under the direction of the supreme artist.

Exploring Catholic Theology, 113–114

What the Bible Teaches

What the Bible teaches is not always reducible to what's in the Bible. What the Bible teaches is what God intends us to know, what's inspired by God through the Bible for the sake of our salvation. To get that, we have to be attentive to the patterns, themes, and trajectories within the whole of the Bible. A good example is slavery. Was slavery part of the scene during the whole period in which the Bible was written? Yes, sure it was, as it was in almost every ancient culture. But is slavery something taught by the Bible, encouraged by the Bible? I would say no, and to get that we look at the totality of the Bible, its great themes. Mind you, the people who opposed slavery in the eighteenth and nineteenth centuries and brought it to an end, both in Europe and America, were precisely biblical people. They were listening to what the Bible teaches, and not simply reading, dumbly, what's in the Bible. I think that distinction is very important for biblical interpretation.

To Light a Fire on the Earth, 172–173

God Spoke by a Son

The claim of the great Abrahamic religions—and something that sets them apart from the religions and mysticisms of the East—is that God has spoken (*Deus dixit*). God is not a mere force or ontological principle dumbly present as the deep background of existence, nor has God remained sequestered in complete and indifferent transcendence. Rather, he has spoken personally to his people. Through the prophets, patriarchs, events, and institutions of Israel, God disclosed his heart to his people Israel. He communicated his passion, anger, tender mercy, and covenant fidelity. Then, in the fullness of time, God spoke, as the author of the letter to the Hebrews has it, "by a Son" (Heb. 1:2). The Word, which made the universe and filled the minds and mouths of the prophets, came finally in person, speaking the compassion that God is. "God is love, and those who abide in love abide in God, and God abides in them" (1 John 4:16).

Arguing Religion, 11 12

The Interpretative Key of Scripture

Jesus is the recapitulation of creation. In his Resurrection from the dead, he heals, renews, and elevates the fallen world. The recapitulating Christ is himself the interpretive key of the whole Scripture, since he is the Logos made flesh, the very embodiment of the *regula fidei* in all its dimensions. When this key is lost, the various pieces of the biblical revelation remain disconnected, or as was the case with the Gnostics, they are assembled erroneously.

Exploring Catholic Theology, 115

The "Inside" View of Scripture

Hans Urs von Balthasar once commented that the windows of a Gothic cathedral are unimpressive, drab, and unintelligible when seen from the outside. Only when one enters the church and sees the light streaming through them do the windows reveal their beauty and narrative density. So the Bible, when viewed from the "outside," from an analytical distance, necessarily appears flat and uninspired, but that same Scripture, when surveyed from inside the life of the Church, through the light of doctrine, practice, and prayer, takes on depth, color, and spiritual power. Again, this is not to encourage naiveté or credulousness in biblical interpretation; but it is to summon the reader of the Bible to respect the distinctively spiritual and ecclesial nature of the documents that she approaches.

The Priority of Christ, 47

THE STORY
of ISRAEL

The Flawed Kings of Israel

The emphasis on Abram's numerous descendants calls to mind the command given to the first king to "be fruitful and multiply" (Gen. 1:28). The royal promise is extended to Abram's grandson. After his nightlong wrestling match with an angel, Jacob hears God: "No longer shall you be called Jacob, but Israel shall be your name. . . . I am God Almighty: be fruitful and multiply; a nation and a company of nations shall come from you, and kings shall spring from you" (Gen. 35:10–11). This royal and fruitful nation, this people set apart to operate according to God's heart, is perhaps best characterized as a "corporate Adam" endowed with the privileges and bearing the responsibilities of the first tender of the garden. The kingship motif continues throughout the Old Testament narrative. Moses, Joshua, Samson, Gideon, Jephthah, and Samuel are kingly, new Adam figures in the measure that they order the people Israel. But even the most cursory reading of the relevant stories discloses that none of these figures are flawless kings; indeed, all share in the spiritual ambiguity of the first Adam, which means that the quest for definitive leadership in Israel is ongoing and open-ended.

2 Samuel, 11

Jesus, the Climax to Israel's Story

In order to proclaim the Lordship of Jesus, we have to know and present the story of Israel in a convincing way. One of the earliest and most dangerous heresies that the Church opposed was Marcionism—namely, the attempt to make sense of Jesus apart from Israel. There is rampant Marcionism today! And this is precisely why Jesus is reduced to the level of an inspiring moral teacher. Jesus is, in fact, the climax to a great story, the culminating act of a great drama. Temple, covenant, law, Torah, prophecy, Promised Land, Passover—all speak of him and point toward him. Speaking of Jesus apart from Israel is like acting in the fifth act of *Hamlet* but having no idea what went on in acts one through four.

"Acts of the Apostles: What Does the Church Do?," Talk

A Beacon to the World

The Lord chose for his work of salvation the people Israel, a family formed after his own mind and heart. By the integrity of their worship and their moral life, they would become a beacon to the rest of the world, drawing everyone back into union with their Creator. Notice please how God sends a series of priests, prophets, and kings—anointed figures—whose purpose is to shape Israel once again according to the pattern of Adam before the fall.

"*Imago Dei* as Privilege and Mission," Talk

Final Loyalty to God

The most elemental expression of Old Testament faith is the Shema found in the book of Deuteronomy: "Hear O Israel, the LORD our God is one LORD" (Deut. 6:4). God's unity was, for the ancient Israelites, much more than one divine attribute among many; it was the defining feature of God's way of being. And monotheism was, consequently, much more than an intellectual conviction; it was an existential statement of the highest import. In saying that the God of Israel is the only God, the people were claiming, implicitly, that nothing other than God commands their final loyalty. No country, leader, political party, culture, civilization, moral ideal, or rival god can compete with the one God.

Exploring Catholic Theology, 152–153

Dreaming of a Messiah

The most heartbreaking and theologically challenging moment in Israelite history was the destruction of Jerusalem, the burning of the temple, and the forced exile of the cream of the society, affected by the Babylonian invaders in 587 BC. This demonstrated, in the minds of the most theologically alert, that Israel's identity and purpose were seriously compromised. This is why Israel began to dream of a Messiah, a new David, a new Moses, who would fulfill the covenant, restore the integrity of the temple, deal with the enemies of the nation, unite the tribes, and ultimately rule as Lord of the world.

"Imago Dei as Privilege and Mission," Talk

David in Full

Adam was not only a king; he was also a priest—which is to say, someone who affects a mystical union between divinity and humanity. After him, Noah, Abraham, Jacob, Moses, Aaron, and Samuel were also, to varying degrees of intensity, priests. Wearing the sacred vestment of the priesthood and dancing before the Ark of the Covenant, King David emerged as David the high priest and hence recapitulated and brought to full expression the priesthood of the work of his predecessors. Samuel's anointing of David the shepherd boy could thus be seen as both a kingly and priestly designation. When the first followers of Jesus referred to him as *Christos* (anointed), they were appreciating him as David in full. The Christian reader will thus see in David the most compelling anticipation of Jesus, the definitive priest-king. Though this sort of move is always hermeneutically dangerous, one could make a good case that the most important interpretive key for the New Testament is found in the seventh chapter of 2 Samuel: Nathan's prophecy that the line of David would never fail and that a descendant of David would reign forever. Not only did this prophecy haunt the biblical tradition that followed it—look especially here at the prophets and the Psalms—but it also decidedly influenced the manner in which the Gospel writers came to understand the significance of Jesus.

2 Samuel, 2–3

The Logos in Israelite History

The Logos, who would appear fully in Jesus, the new Adam, nevertheless made himself visible in a variety of ways throughout Israelite history. According to Irenaeus, it was the Logos who came to see Abraham under the terebinth of Mamre, who visited Jacob in his dream vision, who allowed Moses to see his backside, who operated in the dreams of Joseph, and who spoke so eloquently out of the burning bush. Relatedly, it was the Logos who appeared in the visions given to the prophets.

Exploring Catholic Theology, 56–57

The Gathering of Israel

When Jesus emerged publicly and began preaching the kingdom of God, he was taken to mean something very specific—namely, that the tribes of Israel, scattered by sin, were being gathered. In the second chapter of the prophet Isaiah, we find the prediction, "The mountain of the LORD's house shall be established as the highest of the mountains, and . . . all the nations shall stream to it" (Isa. 2:2). The Israelite hope was that, in the Messianic era, Israel would become a godly nation gathered around the common worship of the true God at the temple on Mount Zion, and that this united Israel would become, in turn, a beacon to the other nations of the world. Jesus' entire preaching and ministry should be read under this rubric of the great gathering.

Exploring Catholic Theology, 72–73

The Longing of Israel Fulfilled

From Abraham through David, Yahweh pledged that he would be Israel's God and Israel would be his special people. However, despite God's fidelity, the covenant consistently came apart, due to the people's sin. What the first Christians discerned was that in Jesus the long-desired covenant was finally fulfilled, that divinity and humanity had indeed embraced, that God's will and the will of faithful Israel had fallen, at last, into harmony. The Word of God's covenantal love, which was addressed to Abraham, Moses, David, Isaiah, and Jeremiah, has now entered into a radical union with the flesh of this particular Israelite, Jesus from Nazareth, and thus, in this Jesus, the longing of Israel is fulfilled.

Eucharist, 78

CHAPTER V

THE
CHURCH

The Church is that society, that Mystical Body,
in which people learn to see with the eyes of Christ
and to walk the path that Christ walked.

Catholicism, 155

THE MYSTICAL
BODY *of* CHRIST

Not a Mere Human Organization

Catholics do not hold the Church to be merely a human organization, simply a coming together of like-minded people, a community of purely worldly provenance and purpose. Rather, the Church is like a sacrament of Jesus and, as such, shares in the very being, life, and energy of Christ. According to the inexhaustibly rich metaphor proposed by St. Paul, the Church is the Body of Jesus, an organism composed of interdependent cells, molecules, and organs. Christ is the head of a Mystical Body made up of everyone across space and time who has ever been grafted onto him through Baptism.

Catholicism, 143–144

Jesus Identified with His Followers

Knocked to the ground and blinded by the supernatural light, the sworn enemy of the Christian community hears the words, "Saul, Saul, why do you persecute *me*?" (Acts 9:4, emphasis added). Saul was intent upon persecuting Jesus' followers, whom he saw as deeply misguided Jews. He had never met Jesus and was confident that the leader of this errant band was safely in his grave. Yet this mysterious Christ insisted that Saul was harassing him personally—"I am Jesus, whom you are persecuting" (Acts 9:5)—a claim that makes sense only upon the condition that Jesus has identified himself with his followers in a manner so vivid and incarnate that when they suffer, he suffers.

Catholicism, 145

Making Christ Present in the World

The Church, to use Paul's magnificent metaphor, is the Body of Jesus, the living organism that makes present Christ's mind and will in the world. It is his love made flesh throughout the ages, his hands and feet and eyes and heart. We are all, through Baptism, members of that Body, hence organically related to him and to each other. Our purpose is his purpose—to carry the nonviolent and forgiving love of God to a hungry world, to go to the darkest places, to the far country in quest of sinners; to be both judge (sign of contradiction) and bearer of salvation.

"Moving Beyond a Beige Catholicism," Talk

Drawing the World into Community

The Lord's calling of his first disciples somehow gets at the very heart of Jesus' life and work, revealing what he is about. He comes into the world as the Second Person of the Blessed Trinity, a representative from the community that is God—and thus his basic purpose is to draw the world into community around him. He said to them, "Follow me, and I will make you fishers of men" (Matt. 4:19). Notice the way that God acts. He is direct, in your face; he does the choosing. Jesus is not offering

a doctrine, a theology, or a set of beliefs. He is offering himself:
become my disciple; apprentice to me.

"The Irresistible Call," Homily

Mother of the Church

Catholic theology has drawn a further implication from Mary's
status as Mother of God—namely, her role as Mother of the
Church. If she is the one through whom Christ was born, and
if the Church is Christ's Mystical Body, then she must be, in a
very real sense, the Mother of the Church. She is the one through
whom Jesus continues to be born in the hearts of those who
believe.

Catholicism, 98

We Don't Go It Alone

We are a missionary Church. We are sent by the Lord to spread
his word and do his work. The Christian Gospel is just not
something that we are meant to cling to for our own benefit.
Rather, it is like seed that we are meant to give away. We do
this work together, with others, in community. Ministers
need people to support them, pray for them, talk to them, and
challenge them. Francis of Assisi had an experience of God and
then, within months, gathered people around him; Dominic,
from the beginning, had brothers in his work; and Mother
Teresa attracted a number of her former students to join her in
her mission. We don't go it alone.

"A Portrait of the Church," Homily

Collaboration in the Body of Christ

In straight Pauline language, we are all members of the Body of Christ, all organs in a Body to whose purposes we are subordinated and to whose health we are ordered. All of us in this Body—priests and laity alike—realize therefore that our lives are not about us. It is, therefore, not for our aggrandizement or for the consolidation of our power that we exist; it is only for the sake of the Body. And it is in this common subordination to a good beyond ourselves that all of us enjoy a legitimate equality: each of us having something indispensable to do and to be for the sake of the Body of Christ.

Bridging the Great Divide, 255

The Mission of the Mystical Body

As priest, prophet, and king, Jesus became not simply the founder of a new community but the organic head of a new Body. Grafted onto him, the Church takes on the task and responsibility of Israel and Adam: to Edenize the world and to restore creation to its integrity. As Vatican II so clearly taught, all of the members of the Mystical Body, therefore, have priestly, prophetic, and kingly orders. All of the baptized are meant to be vehicles of sanctification, instruction, and right governance.

"Imago Dei as Privilege and Mission," Talk

THE EUCHARIST

Three Names for the Sacrament

In his treatment of the Eucharist in the *Summa theologiae*, Thomas Aquinas said that the sacrament has three names, each one corresponding to one of the dimensions of time. As we look to the past, we call the sacrament *sacrificium* (sacrifice), for it embodies the self-immolation of Christ on the cross. Secondly, as we look to the present, we call it *communio* (communion), since it realizes the coming together of the Body of Christ here and now. Finally, as we look to the future, we call it *Eucharistia* (Eucharist), since it anticipates the great thanksgiving that will take place in heaven when we are in the company of the holy ones, at the eschatological banquet.

Eucharist, 60

The Continuance of Jesus' Sacrifice

The Mass is indeed described as an *anamnesis* (a remembrance) of the Last Supper and Calvary, but this term is meant in much more than a merely psychological sense. Since Jesus is divine, all of his actions, including and especially the sacrificial act by which he saved the world, participate in the eternity of God and hence can be made present at any point in time. To "remember" him, therefore, is to participate even now in the saving events of the past, bringing them, in all of their dense reality, to the present day. The Battle of Hastings cannot be re-presented, except in the most superficial sense, since it belongs irretrievably to the past, but the sacrifice of Jesus can. Those who are gathered around the altar of Christ are not simply recalling Calvary; Calvary has become present to them in all of its spiritual power.

Eucharist, 89

No Communion without Sacrifice

In a world gone wrong, there is no communion without sacrifice. Since the world has been twisted out of shape, it can be straightened only through a painful process of reconfiguration. It is practically impossible to read any two pages of the Bible in succession without coming across the language of God's anger, but we mustn't interpret this symbolic expression literally, as though God passes in and out of emotional snits. The divine wrath is a theological symbol for the justice of God—which is to say, God's passion to set things right. In his love, God cannot allow his fallen world to remain in alienation; rather, he must do the hard work of drawing it back into communion. And this means that God is continually about the business of sacrifice.

Eucharist, 62

Eat My Body, Drink My Blood

At the conclusion of the Eucharistic discourse, delivered at the synagogue in Capernaum, Jesus practically lost his entire Church: "When many of his disciples heard it, they said, 'This teaching is difficult; who can accept it?'" (John 6:60). Again, if he were speaking only at the symbolic level, why would this theology be hard to accept? No one left him when he observed that he was the vine or the good shepherd or the light of the world, for those were clearly only metaphorical remarks and posed, accordingly, no great intellectual challenge. The very resistance of his disciples to the bread of life discourse implies that they understood Jesus only too well and grasped that he was making a qualitatively different kind of assertion.

Eucharist, 102

God's Power of Transformation

The substances of the bread and wine change into the substances of the Body and Blood of Jesus, even while the accidents (appearances) of bread and wine remain. This change, unlike anything that occurs in nature, is due to the extraordinary intensity of the divine power, which can reach, as it does in the act of creation, to the very roots of reality. The same God who made bread and wine from nothing and sustains them in existence from moment to moment, can transform the deepest ontological centers of those things into something else.

Eucharist, 120–121

Flannery O'Connor on the Real Presence

At the very beginning of her career, Flannery O'Connor, who would develop into one of the greatest Catholic writers of fiction in the twentieth century, sat down to dinner with Mary McCarthy and a group of other New York intellectuals. The young Flannery, clearly the junior member of this sophisticated circle, was overwhelmed and barely said a word all evening. McCarthy, a former Catholic, trying to draw O'Connor out, made a few nice remarks about the Eucharist, commenting that it was a very powerful symbol. Flannery looked up and in a shaky voice said, "Well, if it's a symbol, to hell with it." I can't imagine a better summary of the Catholic doctrine of the Real Presence.

Catholicism, 192

The Eucharist Christifies Us

Many of the Church Fathers characterized the Eucharist as food that effectively immortalizes those who consume it. They understood that if Christ is really present in the Eucharistic elements, the one who eats and drinks the Lord's Body and Blood becomes configured to Christ in a far more than metaphorical way. The Eucharist, they concluded, Christifies and hence eternalizes. Now again, if the Eucharist were no more than a symbol, this kind of language would be so much nonsense. But if the doctrine of the Real Presence is true, then this literal eternalization of the recipient of Communion must be maintained.

Eucharist, 134

THE SACRAMENTS

The Business of Making People Holy

The Church is about the business of making people holy. That's what the sacraments accomplish. Baptism draws people into the trinitarian life; the Eucharist nourishes them on the Body and Blood of the Lord; Penance restores them to grace when that relationship is compromised by sin; Confirmation strengthens them in the Holy Spirit; Holy Orders and Marriage commission people for the work of the Spirit.

"One, Holy, Catholic, and Apostolic," Homily

The Sacraments Cause What They Signify

Sacraments, Aquinas tells us, are types of signs, since they point to something that lies beyond them—namely, the sacred power that flows from the Passion of Christ. They are composed of a material element—oil, water, bread, wine, etc.—and a formal element, embodied in the words that accompany them. Thus, Baptism is a sacred sign involving the pouring of water and the uttering of the words, "I baptize you in the name of the Father, and of the Son, and of the Holy Spirit," the words specifying the sacred power of Christ operative in and through the water. We can see, therefore, that sacraments are not only signs of grace, but actually the instrumental causes of grace. In Thomas' curt language: they "cause what they signify."

Eucharist, 115

Baptism—The Door to the Spiritual Life

One of the earliest descriptions of Baptism in our tradition is *vitae spiritualis ianua*, which means "the door to the spiritual life." For Baptism draws us into the relationship between the Father and the Son—which is to say, *in* the Holy Spirit. Baptism, therefore, is all about grace; the breakthrough of the divine life; our incorporation, through the power of God's love, into God's own life.

"*Vitae Spiritualis Ianua*," Homily

Confirmation—Strength for Evangelization

Confirmation is the sacrament of strengthening. It strengthens our relationship with Jesus Christ, and it gives us the capacity to spread the faith and defend the faith. It is also described as the sacrament of the Holy Spirit, who is none other than the love that connects the Father and the Son. It is, therefore, the sacrament that gives us the strength of the divine.

"The Sacrament of Strengthening," Homily

Communing with Jesus

Precisely as *spirituale alimentum* (spiritual food), the Eucharist is thus placed in the genus of sacrament. By it, the power of Christ's death and Resurrection flows into us like food into the digestive system. Commenting on the use of the term *communio* (communion) in regard to the Eucharist, Thomas says that through the sacrament we commune with Christ, participating in his flesh and divinity, and inasmuch as we share in Christ, we commune with one another through him. I can't imagine a more succinct summary of the theme of the sacred meal.

Eucharist, 116

Why Chesterton Became Catholic

There is not a greater manifestation of the divine mercy than the forgiveness of sins. When G.K. Chesterton was asked why he became a Catholic, he answered, "To have my sins forgiven." This is the greatest grace the Church can offer: reconciliation, the restoration of the divine friendship, the forgiveness of our sins.

"Divine Mercy," Homily

In the Service of the King

Jesus gathered around himself a band of Apostles whom he shaped according to his own mind and heart and whom he subsequently sent on mission. Priests, down through the centuries—from Augustine and Aquinas, to Francis Xavier and John Henry Newman, to John Paul II—are the descendants of those first friends and apprentices of the Lord. They have been needed in every age, and they are needed today, for the kingdom of heaven must be proclaimed, the poor must be served, God must be worshiped, and the sacraments must be administered.

"Who Will Fill These Shoes?," Homily

Your Marriage Is Not About You

When I was doing full-time parish work, young couples would come to me for marriage preparation. I would invariably ask them, "Why do you want to get married in church?" Most couples would say something along the lines of "We love each other." But I said, "Well, that's no reason to get married in church." Usually, they looked stunned. You come to church to be married before God and his people when you are convinced that your marriage is not, finally, about you; that it is, in fact, about God and about serving God's purposes; that it is, as much as the priesthood of a priest, a vocation, a sacred calling.

"The Two Become One Flesh," Homily

The Sacraments Deify Us

The Mass is meant, at its heart, to bring us into harmony even now with the life of heaven. "May our voices be one with theirs . . ." The Eucharist is meant to Christify us. How important that we don't just hear ethical recommendations from Jesus; we eat his Body and drink his Blood. All of the sacraments have this deifying purpose. Baptism introduces the divine life into us; Confession restores it when it's lost through sin; Confirmation strengthens it; Matrimony and Holy Orders give it vocational direction; Anointing of the Sick prepares us for the transition to our heavenly homeland. What's it all about? Deification.

"Transfiguration and Deification," Homily

CHAPTER VI

THE HUMAN PERSON

Catholicism is a celebration, in words and imagery,
of the God who takes infinite delight in bringing
human beings to fullness of life.

Catholicism, 5

FULLNESS *of* LIFE

The Value of a Human Being

Every human being, regardless of considerations of race, education, intelligence, strength, or accomplishment, is a subject of inestimable value because he or she has been created by God and destined by God for eternal life.

Seeds of the Word, 231

Celebrating God's Delight

Catholicism is a celebration, in words and imagery, of the God who takes infinite delight in bringing human beings to fullness of life.

Catholicism, 5

Becoming What God Meant Us to Be

The drama of human life consists in realizing the full implications of the noncompetitive relationship between the living God and his creation. The French spiritual master Léon Bloy reminded us a century ago that the only real sadness in life is not to be a saint—that is to say, not fully to become the image of God that each of us is meant to be.

"Imago Dei as Privilege and Mission," Talk

The Deification of Humans

The Incarnation tells us the most important truth about ourselves: we are destined for divinization. The Church Fathers never tired of repeating this phrase as a sort of summary of Christian belief: *Deus fit homo ut homo fieret Deus* (God became human so that humans might become God). God condescended to enter into flesh so that our flesh might partake of the divine life, that we might participate in the love that holds the Father, Son, and Holy Spirit in communion. And this is why Christianity is the greatest humanism that has ever appeared, indeed that *could* ever appear.

Catholicism, 2–3

Human Beings Fully Alive

St. Irenaeus expressed the heart of Christian spirituality when he said *Gloria Dei homo vivens* (the glory of God is a human being fully alive). God pours out the whole of creation in an effervescent act of generosity, and then, even more surprisingly, he draws his human creatures, through Christ, into the intimacy of friendship with him. We can sense the beginnings of this divine-human friendship in the Genesis account. Adam and Eve at play freely in the field of the Lord represent humanity as God intended: intelligent, creative, engaged, joyfully alive.

"The Immaculate Conception," Homily

VOCATION

Marked by a Likeness to God

Neither ancient programs of perfectibility, nor Renaissance humanism, nor modern progressivism, nor Marxism, nor the contemporary valorization of freedom have come close to holding up the human person as high as do the Scriptures. For the biblical authors claim that the human being is marked, in every aspect of his existence, by a likeness unto God, and that he has been endowed with a distinctive mission from God, and ultimately destined for life on high in union with God.

"Imago Dei as Privilege and Mission," Talk

The Mission of the Human Person

The *imago Dei* is not simply a privilege in which we delight; it is a mission we are called to undertake. Marked with the image of God, we are like viceroys or representatives of a king who carry documents embossed with the sovereign's seal. We go forth, therefore, with God's authority and empowered for his work. Accordingly, the *imago Dei* is something like the talents that the master entrusted to his servants before going on a long journey. They were not meant to be hoarded or protected, but rather risked on the open market, given away so that they might increase. When we stand before the judgment seat of Christ, he will ask whether we have risked the *imago Dei*, whether we have taught the world how to praise, how to reverence the truth, how to go out vigorously on campaign.

"*Imago Dei* as Privilege and Mission," Talk

A Human Being's Vocation

In a word, the human being's vocation is to lead all of creation in right praise, to name and understand things *kata logon*—which is to say, as they are—and finally rightly to order things so as to preserve the integrity and beauty of what God has made. Could God have accomplished all of this on his own? Well, certainly. But he desired to give his human creatures the privilege of participating in his governance of the world.

"*Imago Dei* as Privilege and Mission," Talk

CALLED *to*
BE SAINTS

The Transfigured Humans

Saints are those who have allowed Jesus thoroughly to transfigure them from within. Paul caught this when he observed, "It is no longer I who live, but it is Christ who lives in me" (Gal. 2:20).

Catholicism, 195

The Church Makes People Holy

Holiness is the integration that follows from placing God unambiguously at the center of one's concern; it is the coming-together of all of one's faculties—mind, will, imagination, energy, body, sexuality—around the single organizing power of God. Or, to shift the metaphor, it is the suffusing of the entire self with the love of Christ. The Church is a bearer of this holiness in its authentic traditions, in its Scriptures, in its sacraments (especially the Eucharist), in its liturgy, in its doctrinal teaching, in its apostolic governance, and in its saints. In all of these expressions the Church is the spotless bride of Christ, the fountain of living water, the new Jerusalem, the recovery of Eden. And by its holiness the Church makes people holy. Indeed, that is its sole purpose, its only raison d'être.

Catholicism, 161

Reflections of God's Perfection

We need the saints in order to come to a richer understanding of God, for each saint in his or her particular manner reflects something of God's perfection. We might think of God as an absolutely intense white light that, when refracted in creation, expresses itself in an infinite variety of colors. The saints reflect particular colors, and this is precisely why their variety is so important in the life of the Church.

Catholicism, 197

Spiritual Satellites

A satellite—a machine of our contrivance—is capable of receiving and transmitting extraordinary amounts of information simultaneously to and from numberless locales. How much more thoroughly and powerfully, therefore, can an intelligence at a higher pitch of reality, in a qualitatively different dimensional system, receive and transmit information. The faith of the Church is that those who are in the heavenly realm participate more intensely in the infinite intelligence of God, that intelligence which embraces all of space and all of time. Can a saint, therefore, receive and send a staggering amount of information? Why not?

"Satellites, the Internet, and the
Communion of Saints," Article

The Powerful Influence of the Saints

Can a saint exert a causal influence on the physical dimension? Can they actually *do* something for us? We mustn't think of the spiritual as simply "other" than the material, as though the two could never interact. Rather, the spiritual contains the physical in the measure that it subsists at an elevated, more ontologically complete, level of existence. Representing the medieval consensus, Thomas Aquinas said that the soul is in the body "as containing it, not as contained by it." Instead of being a "ghost in the machine," as many modern philosophers speculated, the soul, on Aquinas' reading, is *inclusive* of the body. It can move matter, for it is greater than matter. And so the saints, from their heavenly place, can indeed influence, impact, and shape the material world.

"Satellites, the Internet, and the
Communion of Saints," Article

Women of Power

We tend to identify power with office, but genuine power comes from sanctity, power comes from holiness. In the nineteenth century, I've argued, the most powerful Catholics were the "Little Flower" (St. Thérèse of Lisieux) and St. Bernadette of Lourdes. The most powerful Catholic of the twentieth century was Mother Teresa, no question about it. Or, think about a Mother Angelica. Talk about power! I think that's the key to it. Real power comes from holiness, and there's absolutely nothing preventing a woman from becoming holy. Thomas Aquinas was asked, "What must I do to be a saint?" and he said, "Will it." Be a saint, and you'll unleash the power of grace and holiness.

To Light a Fire on the Earth, 70

Exploring the Infinite God

St. Bernard of Clairvaux says that the saints in heaven drink from the divine source and then, in the very satiation of their thirst, they become thirsty for more. Heaven, accordingly, is a delightfully endless process of exploration into the infinite God. Thomas Aquinas says something similar when he asserts that the blessed in heaven, witnessing the beatific vision, are seeing for the first time just how *incomprehensible* God is. What they see in short is not a finite supreme being whose beauty, however stunning, would eventually become stale, but rather the endlessly captivating Black Forest of the divine infinity, a field in which they can play for an eternity.

And Now I See, 136

No Spiritual Mediocrities

The Church is interested in making saints. It's not interested in making spiritual mediocrities. It wants saints.

To Light a Fire on the Earth, 71

CHAPTER VII

HOLINESS

The saint is someone whose
life is about one thing.
Catholicism, 157

FINDING *the* CENTER

Definition of a Christian

Søren Kierkegaard said that the saint is someone whose life is about one thing; a Christian, I would argue, is someone who, at the most fundamental level of his or her being, is centered on the one God of Jesus Christ.

Catholicism, 156–157

The Message of the Rose Windows

The massive rose windows of the medieval Gothic cathedrals were not only marvels of engineering and artistry, they were also symbols of the well-ordered soul. The pilgrim coming to the cathedral for spiritual enlightenment would be encouraged to meditate upon the rose of light and color in order to be drawn into mystical conformity with it. What would he or she see? At the center of every rose window is a depiction of Christ (even when Mary seems to be the focus, she is carrying the Christ child on her lap), and then wheeling around him in lyrical and harmonious patterns are the hundreds of "medallions," each depicting a saint or a scene from the Scriptures. The message of the window is clear: When one's life is centered on Christ, all the energies, aspirations, and powers of the soul fall into a beautiful and satisfying pattern. And by implication, whenever

something other than Christ—money, sex, success, adulation—
fills the center, the soul falls into disharmony.

Bridging the Great Divide, 172–173

Perverted Desires

St. Augustine spoke of "concupiscent desire," by which he meant
a perversion of the will. We have, Augustine said, been wired for
God ("Thou hast made us for Thyself"), and therefore, nothing
in this world will ever be able finally to satisfy us ("our hearts
are restless till they rest in Thee"). When we hook our infinite
desire for God onto something less than God—pleasure, money,
power, success, honor, victory—we fall into a perverted and
ultimately self-destructive pattern. When money isn't enough
(and it never is), we convince ourselves we need more and more
of it; when honor isn't enough (and it never is), we seek honor
desperately, obsessively; when athletic success isn't enough (and
it never is), we will go to any extreme to assure more and more
of it. This awful and frustrating rhythm, which Augustine called
"concupiscence," we would call today "addiction."

Seeds of the Word, 180

To Feed the Deepest Hunger

If the desire for the center, the passion for God, be awakened,
the more immediately pressing desires must be muted, and this
is the purpose of fasting in its various forms. We force ourselves

to go hungry so that the deepest hunger might be felt and fed; we force ourselves to go thirsty so that the profoundest thirst might be sensed and quenched.

The Strangest Way, 63

Christ Calms Life's Storms

Perhaps the most powerful New Testament evocation of holiness as centeredness is the account of Jesus' calming of the storm at sea. As Jesus and his disciples make their way to the other side of the Sea of Galilee, storms blow up and the Apostles panic, fearing for their lives. All this time, despite the roaring of the waves and the tumult of the screaming men, Jesus remains, improbably, asleep. The sleeping Christ stands for that place in us where we are rooted in the divine power, that soul-space where we are, despite all of the vagaries and dangers of life, one with the God who governs the whole cosmos and whose intentions toward us are loving. Even when every aspect of my person is agitated and afraid, that central place is peaceful, at rest. Of course, we see that Christ, once awakened by the disciples, rebukes the winds and calms the waves. This means that the source of peacefulness in the whole of one's person, the spiritual power that can restore calm to the stormiest life, is the inner Christ, the ground of the soul.

Bridging the Great Divide, 173–174

KNOWING YOU
ARE *a* SINNER

Exposed by the Light

Even a cursory reading of Teresa of Avila, John of the Cross, Augustine, and Thérèse of Lisieux reveals that these undoubtedly holy people were painfully aware of how much they fell short of sanctity. At times we are tempted to think that this is a form of attention-getting false humility, but then we realize that it is proximity to the light that reveals the smudges and imperfections that otherwise go undetected. A windshield that appears perfectly clean and transparent in the early morning can become opaque when the sun shines directly on it. Standing close to the luminosity of God, the holy person is more intensely exposed, his beauty *and* his ugliness more thoroughly unveiled. But there is nothing fearsome in this self-revelation; just the contrary, for only what we know and see about ourselves through the graceful light of God can be controlled, changed, or rendered powerless.

Bridging the Great Divide, 175

Windshield of the Inner Life

When you're driving a car in the morning, when it's still a little dark out, your windshield looks pretty clean and transparent.

But in the middle of the day, when the sun shines on it? You notice all the defects and smudges. That's how the spiritual life works. The closer we move to the luminosity of God, the more intensely our inner life is exposed for what it really is.

To Light a Fire on the Earth, 160

Addicted to Honor

In the *Confessions*, St. Augustine tells of an encounter he had on the streets of Milan. He spotted a pathetic figure, a man so drunk that he could barely stand up. Then an insight came to him in a flash: "You are no different than this man!" The drunken man was so addicted to alcohol that his drinking had rendered him less than human. But Augustine was addicted to honor and glory, so ambitious for worldly fame that his every thought, word, and action was devoted to this end. And this capitulation had indeed made him less than human. But then came an even more terrible insight: he was in fact in worse shape than the pathetic street person. For the drunken man would eventually sober up and perhaps regret his excessive drinking, but Augustine had been drunk on ambition for years and showed neither the slightest sign of sobering up nor, until that moment, the slightest regret at his past behavior. There is a tight connection between this encounter and the lines found near the very beginning of the *Confessions*: "Thou hast made us for Thyself and our hearts are restless till they rest in Thee." Both alcohol and ambition are pathetically inadequate correlates to the deepest longing of the heart.

Word on Fire, 101–103

Laying Bare Self-Deception

Many of the spiritual masters can strike us as a bit sharp and overbearing, out of step with the psychological etiquette of our times. Whether it is Thomas à Kempis on every page of the *Imitation of Christ* reminding us that we are flawed, or the Desert Fathers harshly calling us to repentance, or Jesus himself laying bare the self-deception of the Pharisees, the spiritual teachers concur in forcing us to see the truth. Bob Dylan said, "The enemy I see wears the cloak of decency," and an essential part of the spiritual program involves the removing of that cloak.

Bridging the Great Divide, 176

Telling the Truth in Love

Christian speech is true—not only to its object but to itself—only when it is realized in love. John Shea formulated a principle in this regard that is as helpful as it is difficult: criticize someone precisely in the measure that you are willing to help that person deal with the problem that you have raised. If your commitment to help is nil, you should remain silent; if your willingness to help is moderate, your critique should be moderate; if you are willing to do all in your power to address the situation with the person, speak the whole truth. This is not unrelated to Aquinas' point about relating anger to justice: one could be perfectly right in one's criticism, but morally wrong if that critique is not made in the real desire to ameliorate the problem.

The Strangest Way, 107

Hell Is a Choice

Endowed with mind and will, we human beings can respond to the divine love or we can reject it. We can bask in its light or we can turn from it. The choice is ours. God wants all people to be saved, which is just another way of saying that he wants them all to share in his life. But his life *is* love freely given, and therefore, it can be *had* only in the measure that it is freely returned. "Hell" is a spatial metaphor for the state of having freely refused this love, having chosen to live outside of its ambit. Perhaps here we can see the applicability of the traditional symbol of fire. C.S. Lewis said that it is none other than the love of God that lights up the fires of hell. He means that the divine love, when it is resisted, burns us, in the same way that the bright light of day would torture the eyes of someone who had been trapped underground for an extended period, or in the way that a cheerful person would exquisitely annoy someone who is sunk in sadness.

Catholicism, 256–257

We're Not OK

In truly holy people, knowledge of sin is not denigrating but liberating because it enables them to break through the subtle illusions and self-deceptions that finally stand in the way of joy. And the most dangerous of these lies that we tell to ourselves is that everything is just fine: "I'm OK; you're OK." Christianity is a salvation religion, and thus its basic assumption is that there is something wrong with us, indeed something so wrong that we could never in principle fix it ourselves.

Bridging the Great Divide, 175

YOUR LIFE IS NOT ABOUT YOU

I Am Not My Own

My life does not belong to me; it belongs to God. My liberty is not mine; it is God's. My happiness is not something I pursue on my own terms; it is to be pursued on God's terms.

"Moving Beyond a Beige Catholicism," Talk

The Works of Mercy

Dorothy Day once said that everything a baptized person does should be, directly or indirectly, related to the corporal and spiritual works of mercy: feed the hungry, give drink to the thirsty, clothe the naked, shelter the homeless, visit the imprisoned, visit the sick, bury the dead (the corporal works); counsel the doubtful, instruct the ignorant, admonish sinners, bear patiently the troublesome, comfort the afflicted, forgive offenses, pray for the living and the dead (the spiritual works). What Dorothy Day proposes here is an extremely "thick" description of the Christian life. Following Jesus is not, for her, a matter of inner states or private convictions, still less an embrace of gassy abstractions such as "peace and justice." Rather, it is a set of very definite, embodied practices, things that one *does* on behalf of another.

The Strangest Way, 151

A Part in God's Cosmic Drama

We can be critical of any and all social systems because we belong finally to none of them. And this means, finally, that we know our lives are not about us. We are part of a theo-drama the contours of which we can only begin to imagine. It is not the pathetic ego-drama that matters, but rather finding our role in God's properly cosmic drama.

"Moving Beyond a Beige Catholicism," Talk

Finding Our Role

The Swiss theologian Hans Urs von Balthasar speaks often of the "theo-drama." This is the drama written and directed by God and involving every creature in the cosmos, including those sometimes reluctant actors, human beings. On the great stage that is the created universe and according to the prototype that is Christ, we are invited to "act," to find and play our role in God's theater. The problem is that the vast majority of us think that we are the directors, writers, and above all, stars of our own "ego-dramas," with the cosmos providing the pleasing backdrop and other people functioning as either our supporting players or the villains in contrast to whom we shine all the brighter. Of course, our dramas, scripted and acted from the narrow standpoint of the small soul, are always uninteresting, even if we are playing the lead role.

Bridging the Great Divide, 178

A Bit Part in the Theo-Drama

The key is to find the role that God has designed for us, even if it looks like a bit part. Sometimes, in a lengthy and complex novel, a character who has seemed minor throughout the story emerges, by the end, as the fulcrum around which the entire narrative has been turning. In fact, the "main" characters sometimes even fade into relative significance with regard to the great-souled player. That's what I'm talking about in this step; that's what we need to find. When we decenter the ego, and live in exciting and unpredictable relationship to God, we realize very clearly that our lives are not about us. And that's a liberating discovery.

To Light a Fire on the Earth, 163–164

Seeing Ourselves in God's Plan

In his *Abandonment to Divine Providence*, the seventeenth-century Jesuit Jean-Pierre de Caussade encourages us to see every event in our lives—good and bad, fortunate and unfortunate—as expressive of the gracious will of God. When, through faith, we see every moment and every creature as ingredient in the divine plan, when we know that there is a gracious providence at work in the universe, we live in joyful surrender and with a sense of wonder. What is God doing for me now? What path is opening up to me? Why did God send that person, that trial, that pleasure to me just now?

Bridging the Great Divide, 179

SALVATION

Our Only Hope

It is a biblical commonplace that we are unable to save ourselves from sin, since the very powers that we would muster to do so—the mind, the will, and the passions—are precisely what sin has compromised. Our only hope, therefore, is in the divine salvation offered as a gift.

Exploring Catholic Theology, 148

Salvation through Surprise

There was no more fitting, no more extravagant and perfect a way to inaugurate salvation than through Incarnation. God's becoming human was not a merely sufficient means to obtain the end of redemption; it was salvation through surplus and surprise. A gift is wonderful, but it is even more satisfying when it comes as a surprise.

Thomas Aquinas, 46

The Heart of Salvation

Salvation is dependent not primarily on faith but on the quality of our love, especially toward those who are weakest and poorest.

Vibrant Paradoxes, 146

Trained to Be God's Friends

One of the most beautiful and intriguing of Irenaeus' ideas is that God functions as a sort of benevolent teacher, gradually educating the human race in the ways of love. He imagined Adam and Eve not so much as adults, endowed with every spiritual and intellectual perfection, but more as children or teenagers, inevitably awkward in their expressions of freedom. The long history of salvation is, therefore, God's patient attempt to train his human creatures to be his friends. All of the covenants, laws, commandments, and rituals of both ancient Israel and the Church should be seen in this light: not arbitrary impositions, but the structure that the Father God gives to order his children toward full flourishing.

Vibrant Paradoxes, 183

Saved from the Dysfunction of Sin

We are members of the dysfunctional family of humanity, and egotism, fear, violence, and pride have all crept into our institutions and into our blood and bones. Therefore, any attempt to lift ourselves out of the problem, any schema of perfectibility, whether it's political, psychological, or religious, any conviction that we can make it right on our own, is illusory and dangerous. We are saved from the dysfunction of sin only when Jesus' way of nonviolence and love, a path not of the world, appeared in our world.

To Light a Fire on the Earth, 161

Heaven Meets Earth

If we're spiritually minded, we tend to think of salvation as an escape from this world—this vale of tears—to a disembodied state called "heaven." The problem is that these convictions have far more to do with Plato than with the Bible. Biblical cosmology is not fundamentally dualistic. It speaks indeed of "heaven" and "earth," but it sees these two realms as interacting and interpenetrating fields of force. Heaven, the arena of God and the angels, touches upon and calls out to earth, the arena of humans, animals, plants, and planets. On the biblical reading, salvation, therefore, is a matter of the meeting of heaven and earth, so that God might reign as thoroughly here below as he does on high.

Vibrant Paradoxes, 155–156

The Uncanny God of Salvation

The God who comes to us in Jesus Christ, who lifts us up beyond ourselves and moves us to salvation, the God of ecstatic self-offering, the God whose outreach of love is greater than we can think or imagine, is very strange. That, it seems to me, is a valid one-sentence summary of Thomas Aquinas' doctrine of God. What Thomas endeavors to say in his hundreds of pages on God is really quite simple: God is uncanny.

Thomas Aquinas, 61

THE VIRTUES

Discipline of Desire

On display in both classical philosophy and the Bible is liberty as the disciplining of desire so as to make the achievement of the good first possible and finally effortless. Think of the manner in which a young man comes to play the piano freely or a young woman to master the intricacies of the game of golf. Each becomes free in the measure that he or she internalizes the relevant objectivities that govern the disciplines in question.

"Imago Dei as Privilege and Mission," Talk

Spiritual Physics

Every time I perform a moral act, I am building up my character, and every time I perform an unethical act, I am compromising my character. A sufficient number of virtuous acts, in time, shapes me in such a way that I can predictably and reliably perform virtuously in the future, and a sufficient number of vicious acts can misshape me in such a way that I am incapable of choosing rightly in the future. This is not judgmentalism; it is a kind of spiritual or moral physics, an articulation of a basic law.

Seeds of the Word, 226–227

Faith Enhances the Mind

Faith is the virtue in us that corresponds to God's opening of the door to the transcendent dimension. The knowing mind can grasp an enormous range of truths concerning the world of ordinary experience, culminating in the scientific programs of Isaac Newton and Albert Einstein and the philosophical speculations of Aristotle, Spinoza, and Kant, but this move of the mind, no matter how successful and aggressive, can never in principle grasp the inner life of God. That can only be received as a grace, and faith is the virtue by which one intellectually accepts this gift.

The Priority of Christ, 277

An Aching Desire for Good

Hope is an aspiration to a good that transcends any of the goods available within the world. It is born in us only when that supreme Good invades our souls and reconfigures them. The desire for a properly eternal value becomes an existential possibility only when the structures of this world no longer appear as ultimate. The theological virtue of hope is that inchoate, aching desire for a good that one cannot in principle understand; it is, accordingly, quite close to what C.S. Lewis names "joy."

The Priority of Christ, 277

The Very Life of God

Of the three supernatural virtues, the greatest, as Paul specified, is love, for love is the very life of God. Faith opens the dimension of eternity; hope makes us desire it; but love allows us to participate in it, even now. In heaven itself, faith will fade away (for we shall see God's essence), and hope will evanesce (for we will have attained what we had hoped for), but love will remain, because love is what heaven is. The essential dynamic of the divine life is being-with-and-for-the-other. The Father is constituted as Father by his sheer relationality to the Son, and the Son's very sonship is his being with the Father, and the Holy Spirit, as such, is nothing but the mutual interpenetration of Father and Son. To be God is therefore to be love, the willing of the good of the other.

The Priority of Christ, 277

The Supreme Act of Love

Love, in the theological sense, is not a feeling or a sentiment, though it is often accompanied by those psychological states. In its essence, love is an act of the will—more precisely, the willing of the good of the other as other. To love is really to want what is good for someone else and then to act on that desire. Many of us are kind, generous, or just, but only so that someone else might return the favor and be kind, generous, and just to us. This is indirect egotism rather than love. Real love is an ecstatic act, a leaping outside of the narrow confines of my needs and desires, and an embrace of the other's good for the other's sake. It is an escape from the black hole of the ego, which tends to draw everything around it into itself. In light of this understanding, we can now see that God's creation of the world is a supreme act of love.

Eucharist, 28

Supernatural Prudence

In the breakthrough of grace, the natural virtue of prudence is transformed, elevated into supernatural prudence—which is to say, a moral sensibility radically in service of the love of God. The *ratio* of the supernaturally prudent person is rectified, ordered, by the radical desire to be like God, to will the good of the other as other. This is why Augustine can define elevated prudence as the love that well discriminates between those things that foster the tending toward God and those that can impede it. A feel for the expression of divine love in concrete situations is infused or supernaturalized prudence.

The Priority of Christ, 299

St. Katharine Drexel and Justice

What happens to the virtue of justice when it is transfigured by the love that is the divine life? It becomes radicalized, absolutized, elevated, perfected, turning into a total gift of self, a willingness to render to the other beyond what is merely his due. St. Katharine Drexel, an heir to a multimillion-dollar fortune, was so impressed by the needs of the excluded "other" that she gave away the entirety of her wealth and the whole of her life on his behalf. By attending to the dynamics of her choices and moves, we see supernaturalized justice on display.

The Priority of Christ, 317

The Power to Do the Right Thing

The performance of the morally right act is relatively easy when it meets no opposition either from within the agent himself or from the external environment. But there are times in the course of life when we are compelled by conscience to take a particular action even though some threat, perhaps mild, perhaps grave, looms over its performance. To do the right thing would result in the loss of one's job, or the harsh criticism of one's peers, or in the limit case, the forfeit of one's life. The *virtus* by which a moral subject is able to face down those fears is courage.

The Priority of Christ, 281

CHAPTER VIII

EVANGELIZATION

People should be able to see by the way
we behave and think that God is real.
Seeds of the Word, 211–212

MISSION

The Impulse to Mission

No biblical figure is ever given an experience of God without receiving, at the same time, a commission. Moses spies the burning bush, hears the sacred name of Yahweh, and is then told to go back to Egypt to liberate his people; Isaiah enjoys a mystical encounter with God amidst the splendor of the temple liturgy and is then sent to preach; Saul is overwhelmed by the luminosity of the risen Jesus and is subsequently called to apostleship. Balthasar has argued that the beautiful, by its nature, calls and sends: it stops the viewer in his tracks (aesthetic arrest) and then plants within him a desire to speak to others of what he has seen.

Bridging the Great Divide, 49–50

A Christian's Dual Imperatives

The theme of Jesus' "inaugural address" is conversion: "The kingdom of God has come near; repent, and believe in the good news" (Mark 1:15). And the motif of his final words is mission: "Go therefore and make disciples of all nations" (Matt. 28:19). The Christian life is lived in between, and under the conditioning of, these two imperatives. Having seen the form, having been seized by the beauty of revelation, our only proper response is a change of life and a commitment to become a missionary on behalf of what we have seen. In the scriptural tradition, no vision or experience of God is ever given for the edification of the visionary; rather, it is given for the sake of mission. Moses, Jeremiah, Isaiah, Peter, and Paul are visionaries *because they are missionaries.*

Bridging the Great Divide, 19

The Heart of Evangelization

To evangelize is to proclaim Jesus Christ crucified and risen from the dead. When this *kerygma,* this Paschal Mystery, is not at the heart of the project, Christian evangelization effectively disappears, devolving into a summons to bland religiosity or generic spirituality. When Jesus crucified and risen is not proclaimed, a beige and unthreatening Catholicism emerges, a thought system that is, at best, an echo of the environing culture. Peter Maurin, one of the founders of the Catholic Worker Movement, said that the Church has taken its own dynamite and placed it in hermetically sealed containers and sat on the lid. In a similar vein, Stanley Hauerwas commented that the problem with Christianity is not that it is socially conservative or politically liberal, but that "it is just too damned dull"! For both Maurin and Hauerwas, what leads to this attenuation is a refusal to preach the dangerous and unnerving news concerning Jesus risen from the dead.

Bridging the Great Divide, 256

St. Francis Never Said It

Although it's a popular quote, there is little historical ground for the claim that St. Francis said, "Preach the Gospel at all times; when necessary, use words." I mean, I get it. But I'm afraid it's been used far too often to justify an anti-intellectualism and a pastoral reductionism in the Church. Neither is helpful right now.

"Acts of the Apostles: What Does the Church Do?," Talk

Fishers of Men

"Follow me, and I will make you fishers of men" (Matt. 4:19). This is one of the best one-liners in Scripture. God is the Creator, the one who makes us from nothing. And what he makes us is always a reflection of himself: a fisher of men.

"The Irresistible Call," Homily

Prayer, the Lifeblood of Mission

Prayer is not incidental to ministry. It is not decorative. It is the lifeblood of the Church's efforts. Without it, nothing will succeed; without it, no ministers will come forward. At all points, pray, pray, pray.

"A Portrait of the Church," Homily

EVANGELIZING
the CULTURE

Transforming the World

The Church's responsibility is not so much to make itself accessible to the world, but rather to transform the world. It is the mustard seed, the leaven, the tiny ark of Noah. In Augustine's terms, it is the City of God making its way within the City of Man.

"Moving Beyond a Beige Catholicism," Talk

Breaking Down the Walls of the Church

Hans Urs von Balthasar was quite right to speak, in the years just before the Second Vatican Council, of the "razing of the bastions" of the Church—that is to say, the breaking down of the barriers that kept the Church from letting out its transformative energy. This brings us into the heart of a paradox: the Church can perform its mission of world transformation effectively if and only if it has a clear sense of its identity. If and only if it attends diligently to its own walls will it be able to bring its distinctive mode of thought and practice to the wider society. We resolve this paradox far too easily when we say that, since we are meant to evangelize the world, we should ape the world and its style. Robert Frost articulated the proper tension memorably when he observed that "good fences make good neighbors." The Church must know who she is before she can undertake her proper mission of telling the world what it ought to be.

Word on Fire, 206–207

Seeds of the Word

Just below the Parthenon and the Acropolis in Athens is a rocky outcropping called the Areopagus which, in ancient times, functioned as a forum for the adjudication of legal disputes and the airing of philosophical opinions. To that place, some time around 55 AD, came a man who had been trained in both the Greek and the Jewish traditions and who had a novel message to share. The Apostle Paul commenced not with the news itself, but rather with an observation about the religiosity on display in the city: "Athenians, I see how extremely religious you are in every way. For as I went through the city and looked carefully at the objects of your worship, I found among them an altar with the inscription, 'To an unknown god'" (Acts 17:22–23). Christians have long taken Paul's strategy on the Areopagus as a model for the evangelization of culture. Before sowing the Word, one looks for *semina verbi* (seeds of the word) already present among the people one seeks to evangelize. The wager is that, once these are uncovered, the Word of Christ will not seem so strange or alien. In the best case, a nonbeliever might come to see that he had, in fact, been worshiping Christ all along, though under the guise of an unknown God.

Seeds of the Word, ix

Seeing Christianity in the Culture

If the evangelist exercises his analogical imagination, he can see images of Jesus in Superman, Spider-Man, and Batman; he can discern a powerful teaching on the danger of concupiscent desire in *The Great Gatsby*; he can pick up overtones of Jeremiah and Isaiah in Bob Dylan; and he can appreciate one of the most textured presentations of Christian soteriology in Clint Eastwood's *Gran Torino*. Are any of these adequate presentations of the Word as such? Hardly. But are they all *semina verbi*, seeds of the Word? Absolutely. And thus can they, like the altar to the unknown God in ancient Athens, provide a foundation for evangelization, a way in, a point of departure? Emphatically yes.

Seeds of the Word, x

A Transforming Leaven

The documents of the Second Vatican Council speak of the universal call to holiness—that is, the summons of all the baptized to be a transforming leaven in the wider society. The Vatican II Fathers wanted to inspire a generation of great Catholic lawyers, great Catholic business leaders, great Catholic nurses and physicians, great Catholic teachers and writers, in the hopes that such people would carry the holiness they learned in the Church out to their areas of specialization in the secular world.

Catholicism, 150–151

The Art of Arguing Religion

Whatever your perspective on faith in the twenty-first century, remember that there is indeed a middle ground between violent imposition and bland, subjectivizing indifference—namely, the art of arguing religion. The resources of the Christian intellectual tradition—from Isaiah and Paul, to Augustine and Aquinas, to Newman, Chesterton, and John Paul II—are rich, abundant, and galvanizing. They can guide us to a faith that does not operate in a violent or browbeating manner, but still marches confidently into the public space "with fife and drum." They yield a Church that, as John Paul II put it, never imposes its point of view, but rather proposes it with creativity and intelligence. And they lead us to God, who is the answer to the deepest longing of the heart and the most ardent questing of the mind.

Arguing Religion, 111

The Family Transforms the Culture

The family is the place where the objective virtues arc taught and cultivated and from whence morally informed people go forth for the reworking of the culture. When this kingly responsibility is abdicated, other kings, one can be assured, will step into the breach.

"*Imago Dei* as Privilege and Mission," Talk

Embracing the Culture

Jesus should not be construed as one religious teacher among many, but as the Logos of God, the very pattern of the divine mind, the Incarnation of the reason by which the entire universe was fashioned. This implies that whatever is true, whatever is good, and whatever is beautiful in nature or in human culture participates in him, reflects him, and finally leads back to him. Therefore, the Church of Jesus Christ can and should embrace the positive dimensions of whatever cultural environment surrounds it.

Catholicism, 158

AFFIRMATIVE ORTHODOXY

No Finger-Wagging Evangelization

Affirmative orthodoxy means no compromising when it comes to the great teachings of the Church, either doctrinally or morally. But it's expressed in a positive, affirming way rather than a negative and finger-wagging way. That's the trick now with evangelization. We don't start with "Don't do this" and "The culture's wrong over there." We begin with the beauty and the integrity of the Christian thing.

"Affirmative Orthodoxy," *Word on Fire Show*, episode #102

Models of Affirmative Orthodoxy

Chesterton knew the "yes" of Christianity and celebrated it. And certainly Thomas Aquinas also had a very affirmative approach. He was very generous towards those who disagreed with him. He reached out with a confident spirit toward a whole range of thinkers. And so I look to him. He's not a harping, negative thinker. He's a very affirmative thinker. So there are two models, Chesterton and Aquinas.

"Affirmative Orthodoxy," *Word on Fire Show*, episode #102

Engaging Negative Opponents

The very fact that people engage me on my YouTube videos around religious issues means they know something important is at stake. And it might, for them, take the form of, "Oh, I've got to put that thing down." But they know something is at stake, so even if their language is very negative and vitriolic, it's a price worth paying to engage them. So I like this proclivity toward religious debate, even with its dark side. It's worth it.

"Affirmative Orthodoxy," *Word on Fire Show*, episode #102

The Measure of Success

I'm always delighted when someone says, "Because of something you did, I'm coming back to Mass." There's the ultimate goal. You measure success by whether people are coming to Mass, which is the source and summit of the Christian life. Some people say, "Because I heard you, I'm thinking about the faith again," or "You made me see things in a new way." Good, I'm happy with that too, because it means I'm drawing people closer. The ultimate measure, however, would be the Mass. It would be full communion with the Catholic Church and going to Mass on a regular basis, receiving the sacraments, that's the measure of it.

To Light a Fire on the Earth, 114

THE BEAUTIFUL,
THE GOOD, *and*
THE TRUE

Beauty Touches Hearts

The best evangelical strategy is one that moves from the beautiful to the good and finally to the true. Especially within our cultural matrix, so dominated by relativism and the valorization of the right to create one's own system of meaning, commencing with either moral demand or the claim to truth will likely raise insuperable blocks in the person one wishes to evangelize. But there is something unthreatening about the beautiful. Just look at the Sistine Chapel Ceiling or the Parthenon or Chartres Cathedral or Picasso's *Guernica*; just read the *Divine Comedy* or *Hamlet* or *The Waste Land*; just watch Mother Teresa's sisters working in the slums of Kolkata. All of these work a sort of alchemy in the soul, and they awaken a desire to participate, to imitate, and finally to share.

"Evangelizing Through Beauty," Article

Beginning with Beauty

The movement, in short, is from the beautiful (it is splendid!), to the good (I must play it!), to the true (it is right!). One of the mistakes that both liberals and conservatives make is to get this process precisely backward, arguing first about right and wrong. No kid will be drawn into the universe of baseball by hearing arguments over the infield fly rule or disputes about the quality of umpiring in the National League. And no person will be enchanted by the world of Christianity if all he hears are disputes about *Humanae Vitae* and the infallibility of the Pope.

Bridging the Great Divide, 31

Appreciating the Objectively Valuable

What is beauty? Isn't it in fact the *most* subjective of the transcendentals? Wouldn't most people today say that beauty is just "in the eye of the beholder"? My taste for spaghetti and meatballs is a matter of the merely subjectively satisfying. I would never suggest that spaghetti and meatballs have revolutionized or defined my life. I would never dream of becoming an evangelist on behalf of that particular dish. But in sharp contrast to this is the objectively valuable. Can you see how ludicrous it would be to say, in the presence of the Sistine Ceiling, "Oh, that's just not to my taste"? Or to declare, after having heard Beethoven's Ninth Symphony, "Well, it's nice, but I'm just not into that sort of thing"?

"Catholicism and Beauty," Talk

Our Appetite for the Good

Neither wealth, nor pleasure, nor power, nor honor is, in point of fact, the final cause of the will's activity. So what is it? Aquinas concludes that it cannot be any worldly good, for *beatitudo* must be a good that utterly satisfies the appetite, and the appetite within us is for perfect goodness. Human experience reveals clearly that the attainment of even the greatest worldly goods leaves us still wanting more, still unsatisfied.

Arguing Religion, 94–95

The Route to Truth

Beauty constitutes a most important route of access to the truths of the faith. It is, perhaps today especially, the privileged route of evangelization.

"Catholicism and Beauty," Talk

Image of the Well-Ordered Soul

When I was a student in Paris many years ago, I would give tours at Notre Dame Cathedral, and the place became an extremely important sacramental for me. On June 12, 1989, I saw the North Rose Window at Notre Dame for the first time. I returned to that spot every single day until I returned home for Christmas. Here I was a distant and unworthy successor of Paul Claudel, who was converted to the faith while looking at the same window. The Rose Window is an image of the well-ordered soul, the well-ordered city, and the well-ordered cosmos. At the center is Christ, and all of the medallions are connected to that center by spokes.

"Catholicism and Beauty," Talk

Telling the Story

I believe that what is needed today is a compelling retelling of the Christian story. There is, in fact, no narrative more beautiful, more powerful, and more fascinating than that which the Bible in its entirety presents: the Creator of the universe, out of love, has sent his only Son so that fallen human beings might be elevated to share the very life of God. That is a story that will sing to contemporary people just as surely as it sang to men and women of past ages.

Seeds of the Word, 216

SPECIAL
COMMITMENT
to the NEW MEDIA

New Media Connectivity

Look at the connectivity of the new media. I can't think of a better way in human history to reach out to more people and to connect with them. You can not only reach people, but you can share information, share videos, share impressions. You can comment to one another. I can link, in a blink of an eye, to someone all the way across the planet. I can share information, share enthusiasm, share imagery, share videos. I take an iPhone video of an event and then, like that, it can be in Nepal. That capacity to span the globe and to connect with people is just unprecedented. I don't know of any other time in human history that we could have a sense of outreach like this.

"Special Commitment to the New Media,"
Word on Fire Show, episode #77

Getting into the New Media Game

If we don't get into the new media game, then we just get hopelessly behind the curve. We'll just get out-narrated. And then the Christian message won't be heard. Where are young people especially found? They're found in this world; they're found in the internet world. Well, we can throw our hands up and surrender and say, "Oh, that's just a swamp of corruption." Well, yeah, it is in many ways, but we can also get in there with a rival message—and that's what I've advocated now for years.

"Special Commitment to the New Media,"
Word on Fire Show, episode #77

A Breeding Ground of Hatred and Accusation

I have used the internet to great positive effect in my evangelical work for many years; so I certainly don't agree with those who denounce it in an unnuanced way. However, there is something about social media comboxes that make them a particularly pernicious breeding-ground for scapegoating and victimizing. Perhaps it's the anonymity, or the ease with which comments can be made and published, or the prospect of finding a large audience with little effort—but these forums are, increasingly, fever swamps in which hatred and accusation breed. When looking for evidence of the Satanic in our culture, don't waste your time on special effects made popular by all of the exorcism movies. Look no further than your computer and the twisted "communities" that it makes possible and the victims that it regularly casts out.

"The Internet and Satan's Game," Article

Upping Your New Media Game

When someone wants to up their game intellectually and have more confidence in using the new media, I give them advice from Flannery O'Connor. Once when someone observed that Catholics don't read the Bible, she said, "Well, Catholics have two eyes and brains." So, you want to up your game? Great. There's a library of books out there on every aspect of theology. Go and read. Read and read and read and read, the way Fulton Sheen, Origen, C.S. Lewis, Thomas Aquinas, and G.K. Chesterton did. Read and read and read in a careful, selective way the really great texts of the Catholic intellectual tradition.

"Special Commitment to the New Media,"
Word on Fire Show, episode #77

St. Paul's "New Media"

The new media reminds me of St. Paul using the Roman roads, things that were already set up, for the glory of the Gospel. They connected the Roman Empire in a way that was, for the time, unprecedented. And then along comes Saul of Tarsus, who saw the risen Jesus and realized his job was to tell the whole world we had a new Lord. How do you do it? Well, you write things down on parchment and you give them to people who are going across those Roman roads to other cities. And you get on those Roman roads and you travel around what we now call Asia, over to Turkey, Asia Minor, Greece, and so on. Paul was enthusiastically embracing the means available to him. Now we can, quite literally, proclaim Paul's writings from rooftops through satellite dishes. That's just very much in his own spirit.

"Special Commitment to the New Media,"
Word on Fire Show, episode #77

FAITH *and* SCIENCE

Letting the Fly Out of the Bottle

Wittgenstein said that much of philosophy consists in "showing the fly the way out of the fly-bottle"—which is to say, liberating the mind from the narrow and stuffy space in which it has trapped itself for various reasons. Real religion—and not its credulous and naive simulacrum so often critiqued by rationalists—lets the fly out of the bottle and permits the mind to soar.

Arguing Religion, 65

Why the Sciences Can't Detect God

Many respondents to my YouTube videos argue that the sciences don't detect God, and I respond that this shouldn't surprise us. How could a tool useful in the investigation of finite, empirically measurable reality possibly detect the cause that underlies the whole of finitude? I furthermore point out that all of the sciences rest upon a finally mystical perception—namely, that the material world is intelligible, a fact that is hard to explain apart from an intelligent subject who thought it into existence.

"Against the YouTube Heresies," Talk

Suprarational Faith

Authentic faith is not, in fact, infrarational; it is suprarational. The infrarational—what lies below reason—is the stuff of credulity, superstition, naiveté, or just plain stupidity, and no self-respecting adult should be the least bit interested in fostering or embracing it. It is quite properly shunned by mature religious people as it is by scientists and philosophers. The suprarational, on the other hand, is what lies beyond reason but never stands in contradiction to reason. It is indeed a type of knowing, but one that surpasses the ordinary powers of observation, experimentation, hypothesis formation, or rational reflection.

Arguing Religion, 7–8

Christianity Created the Conditions for Science

To hold that the world is created is to accept, simultaneously, the two assumptions required for science—namely, that the universe is not divine and that it is marked, through and through, by intelligibility. If the world or nature is considered divine (as it is in many philosophies and mysticisms), then one would never allow oneself to analyze it, dissect it, or perform experiments upon it. But a created world, by definition, is not divine. It is other than God, and in that very otherness, scientists find their freedom to act. At the same time, if the world is unintelligible, no science would get off the ground, since all science is based upon the presumption that nature can be known, that it has a form. But the world, precisely as created by a divine intelligence, is thoroughly intelligible, and hence scientists have the confidence to seek, explore, and experiment.

To Light a Fire on the Earth, 199

Celebrate Catholicism and the Rise of the Sciences

Just tell the wider story. Think about the number of Jesuits around the time of Galileo who were deeply involved in the sciences. Think about the founders of modern science—Descartes, Copernicus, Pascal, Galileo himself—who were devoutly religious, not just accidentally but devoutly so, with Newton maybe being the most famous. I always cap it off with Georges Lemaître, the formulator of the Big Bang theory, which is now pretty much accepted by all serious cosmologists. Lemaître had to convince Einstein of it. Well, Lemaître was a Catholic priest. That's massively unknown, especially among young people, because all they know is the Galileo myth that the Church is a great persecutor of scientists.

To Light a Fire on the Earth, 104–105

CHAPTER IX

CHALLENGES
to FAITH

Many of the same surveys that provide the raw numbers
in regard to the unaffiliated also tell us why they have
decided to leave the Church, and the reasons are,
surprisingly, theological.

"Address to Younger Scholars Regarding the Instruction
of Undergraduates: Engaging the 'Nones,'" Talk

THE RELIGIOUSLY
UNAFFILIATED

"Nones" on the Increase

Survey after survey has shown that the number of the "nones," or the religiously unaffiliated, is increasing dramatically in our country. Whereas in the early 1970s, those claiming no religion were around 3 percent, today it is close to 25 percent. And among the young, the figures are even more alarming: 40 percent of those under forty have no religious affiliation, and fully 50 percent of former Catholics under forty claim to be "nones." For every one person who joins the Catholic Church today, roughly six are leaving. And even those who identify as Catholic are spending very little time in and around parishes. Most studies indicate that perhaps 20 to 25 percent of baptized Catholics attend Mass on a regular basis, and the numbers of those receiving the sacraments—especially Baptism, Confirmation, Marriage—are in noticeable decline.

"Getting Out of the Sacristy:
A Look at Our Pastoral Priorities," Article

Why Young Catholics Leave

Many of the same surveys that provide the raw numbers in regard to the unaffiliated also tell us why they have decided to leave the Church, and the reasons are, surprisingly, theological. When I first commenced studying these questionnaires, I expected to find a good deal about the sex abuse scandal or about other types of mistreatment at the hands of representatives of the Church, and those reasons are indeed given. But they are far from the most important. Far more prominent are questions concerning the existence of God, the compatibility of religion and science, the relationship between religion and violence, literalistic interpretations of the Bible, and the sexual teaching of the Church.

"Address to Younger Scholars Regarding the Instruction of Undergraduates: Engaging the 'Nones,'" Talk

Evangelization's Top Priority

I've always said that lapsed Catholics are my first target. But a lot of them are lapsed because they've been drawn, knowingly or not, into the secularist ideology. Let's face it, the vast majority of people that we baptize, confirm, educate, and catechize do not stay in the Church. It's an illusion to say, "They're all coming back." To be quite frank, people don't realize that. Our number one focus should be on how to re-engage Catholics who have fallen away.

To Light a Fire on the Earth, 187–188

The Folly of Self-Definition

What was once bandied about only in rather high philosophical circles has now become the standard view of young people in high schools and universities across the West. Subjectivism and voluntarism, brought together powerfully by Nietzsche, Sartre, and Foucault, have become, for many people in our society, especially the young, a sort of default position. Through an assertion of one's will, one has the right to define the meaning of one's own existence. If that language sounds familiar, it is because I took it directly from the Supreme Court ruling in 1992 in the matter of *Planned Parenthood v. Casey*: "At the heart of liberty is the right to define one's own concept of existence, of meaning, of the universe, and of the mystery of human life." That absolutely outrageous statement would have struck Aristotle or Thomas Aquinas as absurd.

"Address to Younger Scholars Regarding the Instruction of Undergraduates: Engaging the 'Nones,'" Talk

From Maintenance to Mission

Pope Francis memorably told us to "get out of the sacristies and into the streets," and to go "to the existential margins." Especially in our Western context, the streets and the existential margins are where we find the "nones." Two or three generations ago, we could trust that many people (Catholics certainly) would come to our institutions—schools, seminaries, and parishes—to be evangelized, but we absolutely cannot assume that today. But yet we still seem to devote most of our money, time, and attention to the maintenance of these institutions and their programs. Might it not be wiser to redirect our energies, money, and personnel outward, so that we might move into the space where the un-evangelized, the fallen-away, the unaffiliated dwell? My humble suggestion is that a serious investment in social media and the formation of an army of young priests specifically educated and equipped to evangelize the culture through these means would be a desideratum.

"Getting Out of the Sacristy:
A Look at Our Pastoral Priorities," Article

Loose-Leaf Doctrines and the "Nones"

A fellow student of mine years ago in a hospital chaplaincy training program was a member of a mainstream Protestant church, and he said one day, with great pride, that the doctrinal statements of his denomination were kept in a loose-leaf binder, since they were always subject to change! An authentic Christianity never hunkers down behind defensive walls, because its purpose is to transfigure the culture. But if it is to accomplish this end, it must be clear about what it stands for and what, by implication, it stands against. We Catholics must be vigilant in this regard, lest more of our own join the swelling ranks of the "nones."

Seeds of the Word, 186

ATHEISM

The New Atheists' Core Misunderstanding

There is so much we could say about the ruminations of the new atheists, so many ways that we could engage them: their obsession with biblical literalism; their deep concern about religion in relation to violence; their conviction that religion is irreconcilable with modern science, precisely because it is a form of primitive, outmoded science; their conviction that faith poisons the minds of the young; etc. But I want to draw attention to one theme that I take to be basic, one misunderstanding that conditions everything else that they discuss—namely, the view that God is a being among many, one cause amidst the range of contingent causes, a reality in the world whose existence or nonexistence can be determined through rational (for them, scientific) investigation.

Exploring Catholic Theology, 18

Atheist Faith in the Nonexistence of God

Almost without exception, the people with whom I deal in my evangelical work think of God as a being in or alongside of the universe, as the highest instance of the genus "being." New atheists Richard Dawkins, Sam Harris, and Christopher Hitchens have rather massively shaped the thinking of young people regarding religion. Here is Dawkins' summation of the theistic point of view: "The God Hypothesis suggests that the reality we inhabit also contains a supernatural agent who designed the universe and—at least in many versions of the hypothesis—maintains it and even intervenes in it with miracles." And this is precisely why he can compare God to a "flying spaghetti monster," a fantastical being for which there is no evidence. In doing so, he is simply aping his mentor, Bertrand Russell, who famously compared God to a china teapot orbiting the sun between earth and Mars. Of course, all of this is utterly alien to the understanding of God on display in classical Christian theism.

> "Address to Younger Scholars Regarding the Instruction of Undergraduates: Engaging the 'Nones,'" Talk

Confines of the "Buffered Self"

My most serious objection to secularism and atheism is that they involve the shutting down of the mind. Though skeptics and atheists both old and new tend to wrap themselves in the mantle of reason, I fear that they are, in point of fact, enemies of reason, precisely in the measure that they drop or rule out of court the most interesting questions. They lock the spirit within the confines of the "buffered self," permitting only certain types of questions—namely, those that emerge within a materialistic framework. Though it is regularly excoriated as superstitious and irrational, religion at its best always represents the opening up of the mind, the full engagement of the *intellectus agens*, and the liberation of the spirit.

Arguing Religion, 64–65

Scientism's Basic Problem

Problems with the scientistic or positivistic method abound, but the most fundamental difficulty is that the entire program rests squarely upon a contradiction. The principle is that the only meaningful statements are those that can be confirmed through empirical observation and experimentation; and yet, that very principle is not confirmable in such a manner. Where or how does one observe or experimentally verify the assertion that meaningfulness is reducible to that which can be observed through the senses?

Arguing Religion, 19–20

The Heresy of Biblical Fundamentalism

Judging simply from my YouTube respondents, the nuanced Catholic approach to the Bible is simply not known. Constantly I hear that the Bible presents a lot of nonsense about talking snakes, a universe that is five thousand years old, and a man living for three days in the belly of a whale. How could any self-respecting modern take any of this seriously? One of my standard responses is to suggest that the Bible isn't so much a book as a library, made up of texts from a wide variety of periods and in a wide variety of genres. Just as one wouldn't expect to take the whole of the library literally, one shouldn't expect to interpret the Bible with one clunky set of lenses.

"Against the YouTube Heresies," Talk

Interpreting Biblical Violence

My YouTube interlocutors often complain about the morally offensive, vain, petty, and above all, violent God of the Old Testament, who commands that the ban be put on cities, who orders blitzkrieging genocide, who wants children's heads dashed against stones, etc. I urge my respondents to read the whole of the Bible in light of Christ, who functions as the interpretive key to the narrative. The image of the Lamb standing as though slain in the book of Revelation, opening the scroll to history, is apposite here. Once that interpretive grid is in place, one can read the brutal sections of the Old Testament in a spiritualizing manner, along the lines suggested by Origen and many others. These stories of brutal conquest and fighting to the death and putting the ban on every living thing are accurate articulations of the ultimate purpose of spiritual struggle—namely, to eliminate all that stands opposed to God. What God demands, in fact, is putting the ban on evil. This makes a good deal of sense to people when one gets specific about the evil we fight: human trafficking, the sexual abuse of children, torture, abortion, etc. Jesus crucified is nothing other than God going all the way down in his struggle against evil.

"Against the YouTube Heresies," Talk

The Heresy of Ecclesial Angelism

Over and again, respondents to my YouTube videos present some version of this argument: "Who are you, a Catholic priest, to be making any truth claims, when your Church has been guilty of so many crimes against the human race?" Then the familiar litany is rehearsed: Inquisition, Crusades, witch hunts (I'm surprised how often this one surfaces), support of slavery, and of course, to bring it up to date, the clerical sex abuse scandal. My arguments aren't so much refuted as ignored in light of this history. My standard comeback is to say that bad Christians don't add up to bad Christianity. Or, analogously, just because Einstein's physics was used to produce the atom bombs that killed hundreds of thousands doesn't mean that the physics itself is faulty.

"Against the YouTube Heresies," Talk

BEIGE
CATHOLICISM

Beige Catholicism

Beige Catholicism is a Catholicism that's become bland, apologetic, unsure of itself, hand-wringing, overly accommodating, that's allowed its distinctive color to blend into beige, so that it's hard to distinguish it from other religions and the wider culture. It was the Catholicism of the post-conciliar period and the poor reception of the Second Vatican Council. It was the Church I grew up in, the church of the 1970s and 80s. It was mirrored and expressed in the literally beige structures we built, that looked like they belonged in a shopping mall and were hardly distinguishable from the suburban environment. That became symbolic for me of a deeper problem, of a Catholicism that's lost its purpose, energy, confidence, color, distinctiveness . . . its sharp edges had been dulled, and its distinctive colors muted.

To Light a Fire on the Earth, 89–90

The Culture of Beige Catholicism

When I recall my Catholic youth in the late sixties and seventies, I think of the color beige. It seemed to be an overriding concern of the teachers, nuns, and priests who formed my generation to make our Catholicism as nonthreatening, accessible, and culturally appealing as possible. Nuns and clergy eschewed distinctive dress and frowned on special titles; doctrinal peculiarities were set aside in favor of generally humanistic ethical values; liturgies were designed to be, above all, entertaining; homilies were delivered by priests who had far more questions than answers; troubling biblical texts dealing with the divine anger and judgment and the reality of sin were scarcely mentioned; Jesus was presented exclusively as friend and brother. There was, above all, a hand-wringing and apologetic quality to the Catholicism of my youth. It seemed as though the project was to "translate" uniquely Catholic doctrine, practice, and style into forms acceptable to the environing culture, always downplaying whatever might be construed as "odd" or "supernatural." Thus, the biblical and theological tended to be replaced by the political, the sociological, and above all, the psychological.

Bridging the Great Divide, 17

The Art and Architecture of Beige Catholicism

This drift toward the abstract can be seen too in the architecture and art of the period. The Catholic churches that were built during my youth fell into an easily recognizable pattern. They were usually great open spaces, cavernous rooms with little color, decoration, or imagery. Altar, ambo, and sanctuary furnishings were simple, blocky, unadorned. If there were statues or Stations of the Cross, they were reduced to the bare essentials, a few lines hinting at figure or gesture. Cultural critic Dr. Robert Orsi has observed that in the hymnals, textbooks, and missalettes of the sixties, religious art had become almost entirely abstract: in place of richly colored and densely textured saints, there were now stick figures and vague shapes.

Bridging the Great Divide, 18

Bleeding into Beige

The culture that is Christianity, the sacred Way, expressed in movement, practice, and apprenticeship, has become, too often, a faint echo of the secular culture or a privatized and individualized set of convictions. The dense texture of the Christian Way has been worn thin, and its bright colors allowed to bleed into beige, and this attenuating has been due to an accommodation to the characteristically modern frame of mind: skeptical, rationalist, and dualist.

Bridging the Great Divide, 26–27

SCAPEGOATING

The Scapegoating Mechanism

René Girard, the great Franco-American philosopher and social commentator, is best known for his speculations on what he called the scapegoating mechanism. Sadly, Girard maintained, most human communities, from the coffee klatch to the nation state, are predicated upon this dysfunctional and deeply destructive instinct. Roughly speaking, it unfolds as follows. When tensions arise in a group (as they inevitably do), people commence to cast about for a scapegoat, for someone or some group to blame. Deeply attractive, even addictive, the scapegoating move rapidly attracts a crowd, which in short order becomes a mob. In their common hatred of the victim, the blamers feel an ersatz sense of togetherness. Filled with the excitement born of self-righteousness, the mob then endeavors to isolate and finally eliminate the scapegoat, convinced that this will restore order to their roiled society. At the risk of succumbing to the *reductio ad Hitlerum* fallacy, nowhere is the Girardian more evident than in the Germany of the 1930s. Hitler ingeniously exploited the scapegoating mechanism to bring his country together— obviously in a profoundly wicked way.

"The Internet and Satan's Game," Article

Reversing a Scapegoating Mob

Girardian dynamics are clearly visible in a story from the Gospel of John. The Pharisees have caught a woman in the very act of adultery. This represents the deep hunger in us for scapegoats, someone upon whom we can vent our frustrations. Excited by their find, they quickly gather around them a genuine mob. They then confront Jesus and seek from him sanction for their behavior, relying, as mobs often do, on established religious authority. Jesus' first move is intriguing. He says nothing, only bending down to write on the ground. One of the most important steps in sapping the energy of a mob is simply not to cooperate. The writing is a wonderful detail—the only time in any of the Gospels that Jesus is depicted as writing. Some of the Church Fathers suggested that he was writing the sin of each of the stone throwers. Then the Lord delivers what is undoubtedly one of the most famous one-liners in the New Testament: "Let anyone among you who is without sin be the first to throw a stone at her" (John 8:7). Having stopped the momentum of the mob by his silence, he now seeks to reverse it. He does so by turning the accusing energy of the crowd back on itself and also by *individualizing* the members of the group. This breaks up the deadly power of the mob.

"Jesus and the Scapegoat," Homily

Scapegoats at the Passion

The Gospels appreciated the Girardian dynamic long before Girard. A case in point is a small narrative within the grand

Passion narrative articulated by St. Luke. The evangelist tells us that Peter, on the awful night of Jesus' arrest, joined a group in the courtyard of the High Priest's house, who had gathered around a fire, warming themselves against the cold. When they heard Peter's Galilean accent, they one by one commenced to identify him as one of Jesus' followers. Knowing full well what this might entail, Peter vehemently denied the charge, but they continued, hungry for a scapegoat. So panicked was the chief of the Apostles that he swore he had no knowledge of the Lord. The Girardian impulse distorts both the blamers and the blamed. How wonderful and strange that Jesus, on the cross, became himself a scapegoated victim. The crucified Jesus demonstrates God's judgment on this deep-seated and dysfunctional instinct.

"The Scapegoating Mechanism," Homily

Forgiveness, Love, and Identification with the Victim

The crucifixion of Jesus is a classic instance of the old scapegoating pattern. It is utterly consistent with the Girardian theory that Caiaphas, the leading religious figure of the time, said to his colleagues, "You know nothing at all! You do not understand that it is better for you to have one man die for the people than to have the whole nation destroyed" (John 11:49–50). In any other religious context, this sort of rationalization would be valorized. But in the Resurrection of Jesus from the dead, this stunning truth is revealed: God is not on the side of the scapegoaters, but rather on the side of the scapegoated victim. The true God does not sanction a community created through

139

violence; rather, he sanctions what Jesus called the kingdom of God, a society grounded in forgiveness, love, and identification with the victim.

Vibrant Paradoxes, 22

CHAPTER X

MISCELLANY

There are in us, as Shakespeare's Cleopatra put it,
"immortal longings," for we are linked, whether we like it or not,
to the eternal God who stands outside of time.

Seeds of the Word, 194

MISCELLANY

Declaring Jesus as Lord

The claim of the first Christians was *Iesous Kyrios* (Jesus is Lord)—and this was bound to annoy both Jews and Gentiles. The Jews would be massively put off by the use of the term *Kyrios* in describing an ordinary human being. Moreover, the implication that this man was the Messiah of Israel—when he had died at the hands of Israel's enemies—was simply blasphemous. And for the Greeks, this claim was subversive, for a watchword of the time was *Kaiser Kyrios* (Caesar is Lord). A new system of allegiance was being proposed, a new type of ordering and lordship—and this was indeed a threat to the regnant system.

"Acts of the Apostles: What Does the Church Do?," Talk

Successors

In April of 2005 the newly elected Pope Benedict XVI came onto the front loggia of St. Peter's Basilica to bless the crowds. Gathered around him, on the adjoining balconies, there appeared all of the cardinals who had just chosen him. The news cameras caught the remarkably pensive expression on the face of Francis Cardinal George of Chicago. When the Cardinal returned home, reporters asked him what he was thinking about at that moment. Here is what he said: "I was gazing over toward the Circus Maximus, toward the Palatine Hill where the Roman Emperors once resided and reigned and looked down upon the persecution of Christians, and I thought, "Where are their successors? Where is the successor of Caesar Augustus? Where is the successor of Marcus Aurelius? And finally, who cares? But if you want to see the successor of Peter, he is right next to me, smiling and waving at the crowds."

Catholicism, 35

Why There's Anything at All

Any cause—however impressive—among other causes is not the reason why there is something rather than nothing. If one were to ask how to make a cherry pie, one would expect an answer along these lines: you would need cherries, starch, dough, the heat of the oven, etc. What one ought never to expect is an answer such as this: you need cherries, starch, God, dough, the heat of the oven, etc., as though God were one fussy cause alongside the others. God is the answer to an altogether different kind of question—namely, why are there cherries, starch, dough, and ovens at all?

Arguing Religion, 78–79

Immortal Longings

Though the materialist ideology around us insists that we are no more than clever animals who will fade away at death, deep within us is the sure sense that we are more than that. There are in us, as Shakespeare's Cleopatra put it, "immortal longings," for we are linked, whether we like it or not, to the eternal God who stands outside of time

Seeds of the Word, 194

Superhero Christ Figures

I can't help but hear an echo of the ancient Christological doctrine of Jesus' dual nature in the latest films featuring Batman, Superman, and Spider-Man. All three of these superheroes are hybrids—combinations of the extraordinary and the ordinary. In all three cases we have someone who, in his lowliness, is able completely to identify and sympathize with our suffering and, in his transcendence, is able to do something about it.

Seeds of the Word, 53

Stronger Than Dirt

Cultivate an attitude of detachment. This doesn't mean indifference to practical realities, but it does mean a willingness to let go of anything—including wealth—that is less than God. Recently, I read a story of a former Wall Street trader who has become an Eastern Orthodox monk. He now urges his former colleagues in the financial world to place a jar of dirt on their desks, to remind them of what is finally important. It's not a bad idea for all of us.

Seeds of the Word, 174

Our Limited Grasp of Reality

The American philosopher William James once compared us human beings to a dog that wanders into a library. The canine takes in the colors, shapes, and patterns around him; he sees all of the books, the tables, the globe, the ink wells—but he grasps none of it, for those objects belong to a world of meaning that his mind is incapable of perceiving. So we see everything that is going on around us, but we *get* very little of it, precisely because all the events that surround us are part of a theo-drama, a divinely scripted play, the plot, movement, and resolution of which remain beyond our ken. To say, therefore, that the world makes no ultimate sense is a bit like James' dog (if he could speak) pronouncing on the uselessness and incoherence of a library.

Bridging the Great Divide, 189

The Lazy Lake of Relativism

Relativism leads to a kind of spiritual laziness. What gives a river its verve and energy, John Henry Newman said, is the firmness of its bank. Knock down the banks in the name of liberty, and the river opens up into a lazy, undefined lake. People might float on this lake, but they have no energy or sense of purpose. This is an apt metaphor for our society, wherein toleration of each individual's program of self-invention is the supreme moral ideal. We put up with each other as we float on our separate air mattresses on the lazy lake, but we have no purpose that unites us in a common effort.

"Relativism and Its Discontents," Talk

When Will Overpowers Intellect

I believe that the most powerful and influential heresy today is voluntarism—which is to say, the trumping of intellect by will. To state it a bit more simply, voluntarism is the view that things are true because I want them to be true. I don't know any funnier (or more pathetic) exemplification of voluntarism than a video that went viral about a year ago. An interviewer, who was a white male about six feet tall, made his way around an unnamed American college campus and spoke at random to students. He asked them, "So if I told you I was a woman, what would your response be?" To a person, every student he spoke to replied, more or less, "If that's what you discern you are, then I'm okay with that." Then he pressed the matter: "What if I told you that I felt I was a Chinese woman?" Again, without hesitation, each student said, "Well, that's what you are." Finally, he inquired, "What if I told you that I claim the identity of a six-foot-five-inch Chinese woman?" At this point, a few of his interlocutors balked, but in the end, they all agreed that they would be fine with that description if that's what he truly felt he was. In their minds, evidently, gender, race, and even height were not objective states of affairs but a function of subjective desire.

Arguing Religion, 37–38

NOTES

i   The *Catechism of the Catholic Church* points out: *Catechism of the Catholic Church*, no. 2684 (New York: Image Books, 1995), 707–708.

ii   "a particular human environment and its history": *Catechism of the Catholic Church*, no. 2684.

iii   "There is an organic connection between our spiritual life and the dogmas": *Catechism of the Catholic Church*, no. 89.

21   "it has always had a healthy hatred of pink": G.K. Chesterton, *Orthodoxy* (San Francisco: Ignatius Press, 1995), 104.

36   "a cry of recognition and of love": St. Thérèse of Lisieux, *Manuscrits autobiographiques*, C 25r, quoted in the *Catechism of the Catholic Church*, no. 2558.

43 "The deepest meaning of Christian discipleship is not to work for Jesus but to be with Jesus": Erasmo Leiva-Merikakis, *Fire of Mercy, Heart of the Word: Meditations on the Gospel According to St. Matthew, Vol. 1* (San Francisco: Ignatius Press, 1996), 424.

66 "Well, if it's a symbol, to hell with it": Flannery O'Connor, *The Habit of Being: Letters of Flannery O'Connor* (New York: Farrar, Straus and Giroux, 1979), 125.

68 "cause what they signify": St. Thomas Aquinas, *Summa theologiae*, Suppl. 35.1, New Advent, 1920, http://www.newadvent.org/summa/5035.htm.

79 "as containing it, not as contained by it": St. Thomas Aquinas, *Summa theologiae*, 1.52.1, New Advent, 1920, http://www.newadvent.org/summa/1052.htm.

79 "ghost in the machine": See Gilbert Ryle, *The Concept of Mind* (Chicago: University of Chicago Press, 2000).

84 "Thou hast made us for Thyself": Augustine, *Confessions*, trans. Frank Sheed (Indianapolis: Hackett, 1993), 3.

84 "our hearts are restless till they rest in Thee": Augustine, *Confessions*, trans. Frank Sheed (Indianapolis: Hackett, 1993), 3.

87　**"Thou hast made us for Thyself and our hearts are restless till they rest in Thee":** Augustine, *Confessions*, trans. Frank Sheed (Indianapolis: Hackett, 1993), 3.

107　**"good fences make good neighbors":** Robert Frost, "Mending Wall," Poetry Foundation, https://www. poetryfoundation.org/poems/44266/mending-wall.

120　**"showing the fly the way out of the fly-bottle":** Ludwig Wittgenstein, *Philosophical Investigations*, revised 4th ed., ed. P.M.S. Hacker and Joachim Schulte, trans. G.E.M. Anscombe, P.M.S. Hacker, and Joachim Schulte (Malden, MA: Wiley-Blackwell, 2009), 221.

127　**"of existence, of meaning, of the universe, and of the mystery of human life":** "THE SUPREME COURT; Excerpts From the Justices' Decision in the Pennsylvania Case," *New York Times*, June 30, 1992, https://www. nytimes.com/1992/06/30/us/thesupreme-court-excerpts-from-the-justicesdecision-in-the-pennsylvania-case.html.

130　**"intervenes in it with miracles":** Richard Dawkins, *The God Delusion* (New York: Mariner Books, 2006), 82.

147　**a video that went viral about a year ago:** Family Policy Institute of Washington, "Gender Identity: Can a 5'9, White Guy Be a 6'5, Chinese Woman?," YouTube video, April 13, 2016, http://youtu.be/xfO1veFs6Ho.

BOOKS CITED

2 Samuel: Brazos Theological Commentary on the Bible (Grand Rapids, MI: Brazos Press, 2015).

And Now I See: A Theology of Transformation (New York: Crossroad, 1997).

Arguing Religion: A Bishop Speaks at Facebook and Google (Park Ridge, IL: Word on Fire, 2018).

Bridging the Great Divide: Musings of a Post-Liberal, Post-Conservative Evangelical Catholic (Lanham, MD: Rowman & Littlefield, 2004).

Catholicism: A Journey to the Heart of the Faith (New York: Image, 2011).

Eucharist (Maryknoll, NY: Orbis Books, 2018).

Exploring Catholic Theology: Essays on God, Liturgy, and Evangelization (Grand Rapids, MI: Baker Academic, 2015).

The Priority of Christ: Toward a Postliberal Catholicism (Grand Rapids, MI: Brazos Press, 2007).

Seeds of the Word: Finding God in the Culture (Skokie, IL: Word on Fire, 2015).

The Strangest Way: Walking the Christian Path (Maryknoll, New York: Orbis Books, 2002).

Thomas Aquinas: Spiritual Master (New York: Crossroad, 2008).

To Light a Fire on the Earth: Proclaiming the Gospel in a Secular Age (New York: Image, 2017).

Vibrant Paradoxes: The Both/And of Catholicism (Skokie, IL: Word on Fire, 2016).

Word on Fire: Proclaiming the Power of Christ (New York: Crossroad, 2008).